The Educator's Guide to Assessing and Improving

School Discipline Programs

The Educator's Guide to

Assessing and Improving

School Discipline Programs

Mark Boynton & Christine Boynton

Association for Supervision and Curriculum Development
Alexandria, Virginia USA

Association for Supervision and Curriculum Development
1703 N. Beauregard St. • Alexandria, VA 22311-1714 USA
Phone: 800-933-2723 or 703-578-9600 • Fax: 703-575-5400
Web site: www.ascd.org • E-mail: member@ascd.org
Author guidelines: www.ascd.org/write

Gene R. Carter, *Executive Director;* Nancy Modrak, *Director of Publishing;* Julie Houtz, *Director of Book Editing & Production;* Ernesto Yermoli, *Project Manager;* Cathy Guyer, *Senior Graphic Designer;* Valerie Younkin, *Desktop Publishing Specialist;* Sarah Plumb, *Production Specialist*

Printed in the United States of America. ASCD publications present a variety of viewpoints. The views expressed or implied in this book should not be interpreted as official positions of the Association.

Cover art copyright © 2007 by ASCD. Illustration by Susan Herron, www.susanherron.com.

PAPERBACK ISBN: 978-1-4166-0611-6   ASCD product #107037   s12/07
Also available as an e-book through ebrary, netLibrary, and many online booksellers (see Books in Print for the ISBNs).

Quantity discounts for the paperback edition only: 10–49 copies, 10%; 50+ copies, 15%; for 1,000 or more copies, call 800-933-2723, ext. 5634, or 703-575-5634. For desk copies: member@ascd.org.

Library of Congress Cataloging-in-Publication Data
Boynton, Mark, 1947–
   The educator's guide to assessing and improving school discipline programs / Mark Boynton and Christine Boynton.
      p. cm.
   Includes bibliographical references and index.
   ISBN 978-1-4166-0611-6 (pbk. : alk. paper) 1. School discipline. 2. Classroom management. I. Boynton, Christine, 1947- II. Title.

   LB3011.B628 2007
   371.5—dc22

                                                             2007026304

18 17 16 15 14 13 12 11 10 09 08 07   1 2 3 4 5 6 7 8 9 10 11 12

THE EDUCATOR'S GUIDE TO

Assessing and Improving

School Discipline Programs

Introduction

In our 2005 book *The Educator's Guide to Preventing and Solving Discipline Problems,* we covered the major components of a positive discipline program for schools. In this book, we've narrowed our focus to the three essential preventive discipline strategies—building positive relationships with students, clearly defining parameters for acceptable student behavior, and monitoring the parameters that are set in place—and to possible consequences to implement when these strategies aren't enough. Taken together, these four components constitute a research-based model of component-driven discipline (see Figure I.1).

FIGURE I.1

The Four Components of Preventive Discipline

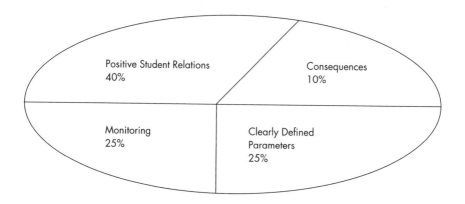

Positive Student Relations
40%

Consequences
10%

Monitoring
25%

Clearly Defined
Parameters
25%

Each chapter of the guide is organized into two sections: one for individual educators assessing their own classroom discipline approaches, and one for school teams evaluating the school discipline program. Schools and teachers can either use the guide in its entirety or concentrate on individual chapters that deal with their specific needs. We suggest looking to the continuous improvement model described by Zmuda, Kuklis, and Kline (2004) for guidance. The model has the following six steps:

1. Identifying the core beliefs that define a school's culture
2. Creating a shared vision by clarifying what the core beliefs look like in practice
3. Collecting accurate data to identify where the school currently is compared to the shared vision of where it should be
4. Identifying what will happen to close the gaps between current reality and the vision
5. Developing and implementing a systemic action plan for change
6. Embracing both collective autonomy and collective accountability in closing the gaps

As Covey (2004) notes, effective systems value conscience over ego: organizational excellence requires high levels of communication and trust, and demands that we manage conflict in positive, creative ways. Yet even effective systems are not free from conflict, and the work can at times be "messy." We have organized this book according to the premise of continuous improvement: although the steps we present are conceptually linear, the leader must be flexible in deciding when to apply them. The focus should always be on the end result—a competent discipline system, defined by Zmuda and colleagues as one that "proves itself when everyone within the system performs better as a result of the collective endeavors and accepts responsibility for the improvement" (2004, p. 19).

We strongly believe that for students to remain disciplined while doing well academically, a competent, courageous leader must be present. Our work throughout the United States has only reinforced this belief. When we encountered strong leaders at schools during building assessments, we always felt confident that they would implement the steps we suggested; on the other hand, when we encountered leaders who were clearly not competent or courageous regarding tough issues, we tended to believe that our assessments were a waste of time. More than ever before in education, leaders must be courageous and willing to lead their staffs in continuous improvement of their discipline programs. We hope this guide will help to facilitate that important task.

CHAPTER ONE

Identifying and Clarifying Core Beliefs

The School Discipline Committee

We believe that every school should have a standing discipline committee to assemble the written rules after obtaining input from staff, resolve discipline-related issues as they arise, and keep discipline on the front burner at all times. The committee should include a representative from each grade level and content area, as well as from classified, specialist, and support staff members. Ideally, committee members should be good communicators and should represent their constituent groups rather than advocate their personal positions. To this end, it is better for constituent groups to elect their committee representatives.

Identifying Core Beliefs

Assessing the Philosophy

Each staff member should assess his or her personal discipline philosophy and submit it to the school discipline committee for analysis. Although teachers can assess their philosophies independently of one another, it is best for them to do so at the same time, in a facilitated setting, using the form in Figure 1.1. The main purpose of the assessment is to find areas of agreement and disagreement among staff members so that they can be proactively addressed.

FIGURE 1.1
Discipline Philosophy Assessment

Directions: For each statement, circle the response that most closely matches your beliefs. If you'd like to elaborate on your response, write a comment.

1. I believe that the most important part of a school and classroom discipline program is prevention.

          Strongly Agree   Agree   Disagree   Strongly Disagree

   Comments:

2. The most important component of a preventive discipline program is developing positive student relationships.

          Strongly Agree   Agree   Disagree   Strongly Disagree

   Comments:

3. Chaos outside the classroom will spill into the classroom.

          Strongly Agree   Agree   Disagree   Strongly Disagree

   Comments:

4. A chaotic school environment is destructive to the school climate.

          Strongly Agree   Agree   Disagree   Strongly Disagree

   Comments:

5. It takes everyone working together to create and maintain a positive discipline program.

          Strongly Agree   Agree   Disagree   Strongly Disagree

   Comments:

6. School and classroom rules need to be proactively taught to students.

          Strongly Agree   Agree   Disagree   Strongly Disagree

   Comments:

7. Supervision of students is everybody's responsibility.

          Strongly Agree   Agree   Disagree   Strongly Disagree

   Comments:

8. Although consequences are critical to any school discipline program, the most important component is prevention.

          Strongly Agree   Agree   Disagree   Strongly Disagree

   Comments:

FIGURE 1.1—*continued*

Discipline Philosophy Assessment

Directions: For each statement, circle the response that most closely matches your beliefs. If you'd like to elaborate on your response, write a comment.

---

9. It is critical to communicate proactively with parents about their children's behavior.

       Strongly Agree   Agree   Disagree   Strongly Disagree

Comments:

10. Students are students first and athletes second; if a student receives a consequence, there should also be a game-related consequence.

       Strongly Agree   Agree   Disagree   Strongly Disagree

Comments:

11. Teachers should be empowered to deal with most disciplinary issues.

       Strongly Agree   Agree   Disagree   Strongly Disagree

Comments:

12. When giving students consequences, it's important to let them keep their dignity and treat them with respect.

       Strongly Agree   Agree   Disagree   Strongly Disagree

Comments:

13. There should be a balance between consequences and incentives or rewards.

       Strongly Agree   Agree   Disagree   Strongly Disagree

Comments:

14. When individual staff members ignore school rules, the entire discipline program is undermined.

       Strongly Agree   Agree   Disagree   Strongly Disagree

Comments:

15. I understand that developing and implementing an effective discipline program takes a great deal of effort by everyone, but the payoff is well worth the effort.

       Strongly Agree   Agree   Disagree   Strongly Disagree

Comments:

Discussing the Results

Once committee members have assessed their personal beliefs, they should discuss and list areas of philosophical agreement and disagreement on a chart (see Figure 1.2). The areas of agreement will form the basis for the school discipline program. The facilitator may want to start this discussion by saying something along these lines: "I want to share with you the results of our discipline philosophy assessment. We will keep these results posted, as the beliefs will form the basis for our school discipline philosophy and for the rules that we will later develop as a staff."

FIGURE 1.2
Sample List of Areas of Philosophical Agreement and Disagreement

Areas of Philosophical Agreement	Areas of Philosophical Disagreement
• Prevention is key	• Supervision is everyone's responsibility
• Relationships are important	• Athletes should be students first
• Structure is important	
• Rules need to be taught	
• There should be a balance between consequences and rewards	

Resolving Areas of Disagreement

Teachers who don't believe in a policy will probably not do their part to support it, and in some cases may even sabotage it. As committee members discuss the norms, they begin to understand each other's points of view, even if they don't agree with them. In some cases, a better alternative arises after hearing the pros and cons of a stated belief. Both individuals and organizations grow in reciprocity with others as they resolve differences, listen to one another, and achieve consensus.

Without open, honest discussion of important issues, educators cannot identify and deal with barriers as policies emerge. For this reason, it is important to find out where the areas of disagreement are and to work through them. Before doing so, however, it is helpful to first establish norms of collaboration that clearly articulate how staff members should work together. We recommend that these operating norms be reviewed with staff and used whenever emotionally charged discussions are conducted.

Let's imagine a scenario in which half the staff agrees that supervision is everyone's responsibility, and the other half believes it's exclusively the administration's responsibility. The facilitator should review the operating norms with the staff and post them for reference. He or she may begin the process by saying something like this: "As we have discussed before, when we hold discussions that are potentially charged with differing opinions and strong beliefs, we will follow our operating norms. I have them posted so we can refer to them, and at the end of the discussion we will review which ones we stuck to and which ones we need to focus on in the future. Do any of you have questions or need clarification regarding these norms?"

Conducting a Force Field Analysis

When discussing a controversial policy or belief, we recommend employing Lewin's (1935) "force field analysis" technique, as it helps staff members reduce opposition to proposed changes and strengthen support for them by following these steps (see Figures 1.3 and 1.4 for completed examples):

1. Write down the belief under consideration on a piece of paper.
2. Create a two-column table, with the first column labeled "Driving Forces" (i.e., forces for change) and the second column labeled "Restraining Forces" (i.e., forces against change).
3. List the driving forces supporting the belief in the first column, giving each staff member an opportunity to contribute.
4. List the restraining forces against the belief in the second column, giving each staff member an opportunity to contribute.

In the example in Figure 1.3, the group might want to go no further, as the driving forces far exceed the restraining forces.

Figure 1.4 shows how the committee could go further and change the equilibrium in the following belief statement: "If student athletes receive a consequence for a serious rule violation, they should not be able to participate in the next athletic contest." In this example, the

FIGURE 1.3
Sample Force Field Analysis #1

Belief: It's everyone's job to supervise students in the halls, at lunch, in the bus zone, and before and after school.

Driving Forces	Restraining Forces
• There are only two building administrators and 60 staff members. If we share the load, no one is overworked. • We have over 900 students in this building. You tell me how it's possible for two administrators alone to ensure staff visibility. It can't be done unless we all share the load. • It's more work for us to be visible, but if we don't try we're going to have that much more work resulting from poor visibility.	• Lack of time • Lack of supervision pay

restraining and driving forces are closer to equilibrium; changing the balance in favor of the driving forces could help increase support for the policy.

Changing the Equilibrium

The balance in a force field analysis can be changed by discussing how to mitigate each of the restraining forces positively and proactively. For example, to keep parents and teachers from becoming angry as mentioned in Figure 1.4, the discipline committee may decide to communicate the reason for the "game-related consequences" policy as thoroughly as possible, pointing out the driving forces.

Force field analysis helps staff members to articulate their positions, listen to the other side, and collaborate on school policies. Even when staff members don't totally agree with the end result, the analytical process will help them to articulate their feelings and beliefs.

Reviewing the Norms

After walking group members through a force field analysis, the facilitator should ask them to evaluate whether or not they followed

FIGURE 1.4
Sample Force Field Analysis #2

Belief: If student athletes receive a consequence for a serious rule violation, they should not be able to participate in the next athletic contest.

Driving Forces	Restraining Forces
• Athletes are role models for other students.	• Two consequences for the same violations constitute "double jeopardy."
• The prospect of a game-related consequence is an incentive to work on academics.	• The policy unfairly targets athletes.
• The policy emphasizes the importance of being a good, responsible student.	• The policy angers parents and coaches.

the operating norms. For example: "Now that we have gone through this process, let's assess how we did following our norms. As you look at the list, what are the one or two norms that you think we did a good job on today? What are one or two norms that we didn't do so well on and should focus on for our next discussion?" This process can be brief, but it is important as it lets everyone know that these norms are expectations for how the group should work together and that they will be monitored by the whole group.

Creating a Shared Vision

To make it clear that discipline is everyone's responsibility, the facilitator should clearly articulate what staff members can expect from him or her, and what the facilitator expects from them. Following the analysis in Figure 1.3, for example, the facilitator might say the following:

"We've been talking about student supervision, and I'm pleased that we all agree it's very important for students to be supervised inside and outside of the classroom throughout the day. Every morning that I'm at school and not in a meeting, you can expect to see me supervising students as they enter the building and go to class. I will also supervise students when they leave the building and during passing periods. At the same time, I expect all staff members to be in their assigned areas at the assigned times as noted on the supervision schedule. If for some reason you can't be at your assigned location, I expect you to find someone to take your place. If you have any trouble, contact me and I will provide assistance."

This example should be followed for each of the beliefs that staff members disagree with in the force field analysis. Once disagreements are resolved, it's time to clearly state the staff's collective beliefs regarding discipline. Let's say that as a result of conducting the philosophy assessment and holding these discussions, the following collective beliefs emerge:

- Prevention is the key to school discipline.
- Relationships are an important component in a prevention-based discipline program.
- Structure in and out of the classroom is important in maintaining strong levels of discipline.
- Classroom and building rules need to be taught to mastery.
- Supervision is everyone's responsibility.
- Athletes should be students first.
- There should be a balance between consequences and rewards.

These beliefs should be formalized and posted in a visible place as the staff continues to work together to develop the specific rules and policies. One way to formalize the beliefs is to put them at the beginning of the student, staff, and parent handbooks and label them as "Staff Core Beliefs Regarding Discipline." Always date such documents, as they should be reviewed and updated on a regular basis. Another good idea is to review these policies and beliefs at back-to-school night and during parent-teacher conferences. Also, when interviewing potential new staff members, make sure to ask about their core beliefs regarding discipline, to ensure that they align with the school's.

After assessing staff members' core beliefs and creating a collective vision of what discipline should be in the school, the committee can begin to assess the current state of the school discipline program.

CHAPTER TWO

Classroom and Building Discipline Assessment

It is vital that members of the discipline committee identify the current level of student discipline at their school by analyzing multiple sources, including test scores, demographic data, interviews, observations, and surveys. In a competent system, assumptions should be based on reality rather than on a perceived reality.

Assessing Classroom Discipline

To be most effective, teachers should self-assess the current levels of discipline in each of their classrooms. In an ideal environment based on mutual trust and respect, these self-assessments would be shared with the principal, who can then support the teachers' improvement efforts (such as by releasing them to observe other teachers who successfully implement specific goals). Sharing the results with the principal is not absolutely necessary for improvements to happen, however; what *is* critical is for the teachers to set and monitor goals based on the self-assessment results.

The best time for teachers to self-assess is in the summer or fall, so that they can set goals for the upcoming year. Teachers may use the surveys in Figures 2.1–2.4 for this purpose. On these surveys, they can add up the scores in each area and multiply by 10 for a percentage score. A score of 10–40 percent signifies an area needing attention; 50–60 percent signifies an acceptable level of achievement; and 70–100 percent signifies an area of strength. The self-assessment surveys are based on the four critical components of an effective discipline program: relationships,

FIGURE 2.1
Teacher Discipline Self-Assessment: Relationships

Directions: Rate your performance in each of these areas on a scale of 1 to 10, with 1 meaning "Seldom" and 10 meaning "Always."

Staff Relationships	Score
1. I treat all colleagues with dignity and respect.	
2. I participate in all efforts to establish and maintain an effective school discipline program.	
3. I actively and consistently support school policies.	
4. When my students have discipline problems, I work collaboratively with colleagues to resolve the issues and develop plans.	
5. I greet my colleagues with a smile each day.	
6. I compliment my colleagues and congratulate them for their successes and achievements.	
7. I am flexible and willing to look at "the big picture" when my colleagues have a need or concern.	
8. When working in groups, I keep an open mind and consider the needs of everyone.	
9. I am flexible and willing to make adjustments in my schedule and program if it meets the needs of colleagues or the school as a whole.	
10. Staff members consider me to be a positive person.	
Total score:	

Parent Relationships	Score
1. When any of my students have significant discipline issues, I inform their parents in a timely manner.	
2. When any of my students have significant discipline issues, I consistently strive to work with their parents to develop effective plans and interventions.	
3. I proactively contact the parents of all my students to share positive information with them.	
4. I share my classroom rules with all of my students' parents at the beginning of the school year and follow up as needed.	
5. I let parents know when their children have done well or are being recognized.	

FIGURE 2.1—*continued*

Teacher Discipline Self-Assessment: Relationships

Directions: Rate your performance in each of these areas on a scale of 1 to 10, with 1 meaning "Seldom" and 10 meaning "Always."

Parent Relationships	Score
6. When meeting with parents, I begin each conference by saying something positive about the student.	
7. I encourage parents to become involved in the effort to educate their children.	
8. When interacting with parents, I communicate the message that the best way to educate students is for the school and the parents to work together.	
9. At the beginning of the year, I send home a welcome letter that lets parents know the school's phone number and the best times to call.	
10. When parents attempt to reach me, I get back to them as quickly as possible.	
Total score:	

Student Relationships	Score
1. I do a good job of fostering student pride.	
2. I treat all of my students with dignity and respect.	
3. I form strong, positive relationships with all of my students.	
4. I welcome students as they enter my classroom each day.	
5. When giving students consequences, I always let them keep their dignity.	
6. I hold no grudges when students break rules.	
7. I take a personal interest in all of my students.	
8. I communicate positive expectations to all of my students.	
9. Overall, my students treat each other with respect.	
10. Overall, my students treat staff members with respect.	
Total score:	

clearly defined parameters of acceptable student behaviors, monitoring skills, and consequences. We recommend that teachers take all four self-assessment surveys so they can examine the components individually and then compile the results to get the whole picture.

Component 1: Relationships

The most prominent component of a discipline program should be relationships. Students, parents, and staff members are much more willing to comply with directives and requests when they know that we care for and respect them. Although relationships with students are the primary focus of teachers, relationships with other members of the education team are also vital to the climate and culture of the building. We have worked with schools where relationships among staff members are so strained that it is difficult, if not impossible, to work together to formulate a common philosophy or approach. Such conflicts need to be dealt with so that the school's focus can remain on student learning. To quote Lencioni (2002), "If you could get all the people in an organization rowing in the same direction, you could dominate any industry, in any market, against any competition, at any time" (p. vii).

Component 2: Parameters

Establishing and teaching clearly defined parameters of acceptable student behaviors is critical to classroom discipline. Teachers should teach their classroom discipline plan and rules of conduct. The discipline plan applies to all students at all times in all locations, and rules of conduct apply to specific locations and events. Rules of conduct are divided into three categories: academic, classroom routine, and special situation rules. (Steps for determining, teaching, and enforcing the classroom discipline plan and rules of conduct are thoroughly reviewed in our 2005 book, *The Educator's Guide to Preventing and Solving Discipline Problems.*)

Component 3: Monitoring Skills

The appropriate use of monitoring skills promotes positive changes in student behaviors while allowing students to maintain their dignity.

Effectively using monitoring skills communicates the critical message that the teacher is aware of and cares about what every student is doing at all times, and that inappropriate behaviors will not be tolerated.

FIGURE 2.2
Teacher Discipline Self-Assessment: Parameters

Directions: Rate your performance in each of these areas on a scale of 1 to 10, with 1 meaning "Seldom" and 10 meaning "Always."

	Score
1. I teach my academic rules of conduct until all students consistently comply with them.	
2. I teach my classroom rules of conduct until all students consistently comply with them.	
3. I teach my special situation rules of conduct until all students consistently comply with them.	
4. I teach my classroom discipline plan until all students consistently comply with it.	
5. I teach the school rules until all students consistently comply with them.	
6. I test my students to be certain they understand my classroom discipline plan and rules of conduct.	
7. Whenever students seem to have forgotten the classroom rules, I reteach them.	
8. When teaching the classroom discipline plan and rules of conduct, I review the reasons for each rule.	
9. I realize that the first thing students want to know about me when they enter my classroom is what rules and policies I will be enforcing.	
10. I realize that if I do not teach my classroom discipline plan and rules of conduct, the students will test me to see what they can get away with.	
Total score:	

FIGURE 2.3
Teacher Discipline Self-Assessment: Monitoring

Directions: Rate your performance in each of these areas on a scale of 1 to 10, with 1 meaning "Seldom" and 10 meaning "Always."

	Score
1. I consistently and effectively use monitoring skills in my classroom with all of my students.	
2. I am visible in the halls during transition periods.	
3. I monitor my students' behaviors in assemblies.	
4. I stand by the door as my students enter the classroom.	
5. I move around the room during teacher-led instruction and independent seatwork.	
6. My students understand that I am aware of what they are doing at all times in the classroom.	
7. My students realize that I care about what they are doing throughout the building.	
8. During teacher-led instruction, I do not hesitate to use monitoring skills when I see that a student is off task or behaving inappropriately.	
9. During independent seatwork, I do not hesitate to use monitoring skills when students are off task or behaving inappropriately.	
10. All my students are aware of my presence the entire time they are in my classroom.	
Total score:	

Component 4: Consequences

No matter how many prevention-based approaches teachers use, there will always be a need for meaningful consequences. To be effective, consequences must be timely, easy to implement, impossible to skip, and varied enough to fit different types of rule violations.

After completing the surveys in Figures 2.1–2.4, teacher should add up the four total scores and divide by four for a total discipline assessment score. Scores below 50 percent indicate a need to set goals regarding classroom discipline, scores between 50 and 60 percent indicate an

FIGURE 2.4

Classroom Teacher Discipline Self-Assessment: Consequences

Directions: Rate your performance in each of these areas on a scale of 1 to 10, with 1 meaning "Seldom" and 10 meaning "Always."

	Score
1. I consistently deliver pretaught consequences when students violate rules.	
2. I select consequences that suit the violation at hand.	
3. Prior to delivering a consequence, I make certain that I am calm and unemotional.	
4. When I deliver consequences, I always allow my students to keep their dignity.	
5. When I deliver consequences, I never communicate to students that I expect them to get into trouble.	
6. When I deliver consequences, I never communicate to students that I enjoy doing so.	
7. After delivering consequences, I always welcome the students back and hold no grudges.	
8. I discipline students based on what they do, not on their reputations.	
9. I know and follow the school procedures for making office referrals.	
10. I know and follow the school procedures for delivering consequences.	
Total score:	

acceptable level of classroom discipline, and scores between 70 and 100 percent indicate a strong level of classroom discipline. After completing the surveys and tallying the total score, teachers should develop improvement goals for their classroom discipline plans. These are discussed at greater length in Chapters 3–6.

Ideally, teachers will be reflective enough to complete the surveys honestly. If the principal is concerned with a teacher's classroom management skills and doesn't think that the teacher is capable of an honest self-assessment, the surveys can function as guidelines for classroom observation, and the results can be used to write the teacher's summative evaluation and set goals for improvement. (This process is discussed further in Chapter 7.)

Assessing School Discipline

Just as it is important for individual teachers to evaluate their levels of classroom discipline, it is also important for administrators to evaluate the discipline level buildingwide. To do so, they should collect data identifying where the school currently is compared to the shared vision of where it should be. Data can include test scores, demographics, interviews, observations, and surveys. This process takes courage and leadership from the building leader, working together with staff and the school community. The goal is to attain honest, specific feedback regarding all aspects of the school's discipline system. Sometimes information will be attained that is hard to accept, but the knowledge of specific problem areas will help the entire building improve. No system is perfect, but every system can strive to get better.

The staff member, parent, and student surveys in Figures 2.5–2.8 are valuable tools in this assessment process. As in the teacher self-assessment surveys, these surveys are divided into the four critical components of an effective school discipline program. We believe it is important to check the perceptions of all groups in the assessment process, as the differences among them can yield important information. For example, if every group except parents believes that there are strong programs devoted to student recognition at the school, then perhaps parents need to be better informed about such programs, or programs need to be added that recognize more students. Parent surveys can be handed out and completed during conferences at school; as many parents as possible should have an opportunity to fill them out.

The student surveys can be filled out by all students or by students selected at random. Be sure to gather the results immediately, so that students aren't able to plan their responses. The survey in Figure 2.7 is intended for use with secondary students; the one in Figure 2.8 can be used either with primary students or with special education students.

For each statement in the staff member and parent surveys, a score of 5–6 is within the acceptable range, a score of 7–10 signifies an area of strength, and a score below 5 signifies an area needing improvement.

FIGURE 2.5
School Discipline Assessment: Staff

Directions: Rate your performance in each of these areas on a scale of 1 to 10, with 1 meaning "Needs Improvement" and 10 meaning "We do well." If you wish to add comments on any of these areas, please do so at the end of the survey.

Relationships	Score
1. Our school has effective programs and strategies in place to develop student pride buildingwide.	
2. Our school maintains an effective buildingwide focus on recognizing student achievement.	
3. Our school does an effective job of letting parents know when students have done well or are being recognized.	
4. Overall, our students treat each other with respect.	
5. Overall, our students treat staff members with respect.	
6. Overall, staff members treat students with respect.	
7. Staff members emphasize the importance of letting students maintain their dignity at all times.	
8. Overall, staff members treat each other with dignity and respect.	
9. All staff members understand that everyone must participate in the effort to establish an effective school discipline program.	
10. All staff members treat all parents with respect.	
Total score:	

Parameters	Score
11. All staff members have had an opportunity to help formulate the school rules.	
12. All staff members know what the school rules are.	
13. All staff members are given regular opportunities to assess the school discipline system.	
14. Staff members have done an effective job of teaching students the school rules.	
15. Staff members know which violations warrant office referrals.	
Total score:	

FIGURE 2.5—*continued*

School Discipline Assessment: Staff

Directions: Rate your performance in each of these areas on a scale of 1 to 10, with 1 meaning "Needs Improvement" and 10 meaning "We do well." If you wish to add comments on any of these areas, please do so at the end of the survey.

Monitoring	Score
16. Staff members understand the importance of maintaining a high level of visibility buildingwide throughout the day.	
17. Administrators maintain a high level of visibility buildingwide throughout the day.	
18. All staff members actively support the school rules.	
19. All staff members understand that it is critical for them to intervene anytime and anywhere they see a student violate a rule.	
20. All staff members, including support staff and paraeducators, understand that they must actively participate in the enforcement of a structured and orderly school climate.	
21. Staff members monitor student behavior during assemblies.	
22. Staff members monitor student behavior during lunch.	
23. Staff members monitor student behavior during recess and intramural events.	
24. Staff members monitor student behavior in the hallways.	
25. Staff members monitor student behavior before and after school.	
Total score:	

Consequences	Score
26. Staff members deliver consequences to all students, not just their own.	
27. Consequences are impossible for students to skip.	
28. Consequences are timely.	
29. Consequences are varied enough to suit rule violations of differing severity.	
30. Consequences are easy to implement.	
31. When students are referred to the office, communication between staff members and administration is timely and meaningful.	

FIGURE 2.5—*continued*
School Discipline Assessment: Staff

Directions: Rate your performance in each of these areas on a scale of 1 to 10, with 1 meaning "Needs Improvement" and 10 meaning "We do well." If you wish to add comments on any of these areas, please do so at the end of the survey.

Consequences	Score
32. When students are referred to the office, the consequences they receive are timely and meaningful.	
33. Staff members have reviewed the guidelines for what constitutes an appropriate office referral.	
34. Staff members do not overuse office referrals.	
35. Staff members understand that the office is not a "holding area" for students.	
Total score:	

36. We need to consider implementing or improving the effectiveness of the following (please circle "Yes" or "No"):

Processing:	Yes	No
Lunch detention:	Yes	No
Recess detention:	Yes	No
After-school detention:	Yes	No
Friday school:	Yes	No

37. The two or three greatest strengths at our school in the area of discipline are (please fill in):

_____

_____

_____

38. The two or three greatest needs at our school in the area of discipline are (please fill in):

_____

_____

_____

39. Other comments, concerns, or suggestions:

_____

_____

_____

FIGURE 2.6
School Discipline Assessment: Parents

Directions: Rate the performance of your child's school in each of these areas on a scale of 1 to 10, with 1 meaning "Seldom" and 10 meaning "Always." (If you do not know the answer, write "NR.") If you wish to add comments on any of these areas, please do so at the end of the survey.

	Score
1. Staff members appear committed to recognizing student achievement and developing pride in success.	
2. Staff members appear to do a good job of enforcing school rules.	
3. Staff members contact parents in a timely manner when discipline issues develop.	
4. Administrators contact parents in a timely manner when discipline issues develop.	
5. Administrators deliver quick and meaningful consequences during office referrals.	
6. Staff members are visible buildingwide throughout the day.	
7. Staff members share the school rules with parents.	
8. The principal's office does not appear to be filled with students in trouble.	
9. Student behavior at assemblies is appropriate.	
10. Student behavior during lunch is appropriate.	
11. I know that my student's safety is a priority at school.	
12. I feel comfortable contacting my student's teacher if I have concerns about his or her safety.	
13. I feel comfortable contacting the school principal if I have concerns about discipline at the school.	
14. I believe that the rules are fair and appropriate at my student's school.	
15. My student believes that his or her school maintains a safe and structured environment.	
Total score:	

16. Other comments, concerns, or suggestions:

_____

_____

_____

_____

FIGURE 2.7

School Discipline Assessment: Secondary Students

	True	False
1. Students are proud of our school.		
2. Our school provides meaningful student recognition programs.		
3. Students know and understand the school rules.		
4. Our parents know the school rules.		
5. When students get in trouble, our school calls their parents.		
6. Students treat each other with respect at our school.		
7. Staff members treat students with respect at our school.		
8. Consequences are delivered with the dignity and respect of students in mind.		
9. Students know what kinds of behaviors will result in office referrals.		
10. Staff members are visible throughout the school.		
11. Students behave well during assemblies.		
12. Students behave well during lunch.		
13. Students behave well during intramural activities.		
14. Students behave well in the hallways.		
15. Students are rarely tardy.		
16. Very few students act like bullies at school.		
17. Our school provides appropriate consequences for student misbehaviors.		
18. All the teachers at our school enforce the school rules.		
19. Staff members have taught the school rules to students.		
20. Students at our school are unable to skip the consequences they receive when they break rules.		
21. When students break rules, they know that they will receive a timely consequence.		

FIGURE 2.7—*continued*

School Discipline Assessment: Secondary Students

22. The two or three greatest strengths at our school in the area of discipline are (please fill in):

_____

_____

_____

23. The two or three greatest needs at our school in the area of discipline are (please fill in):

_____

_____

_____

24. Other comments, concerns, or suggestions:

_____

_____

_____

Total student scores can be calculated by dividing the number of "true" answers by 21 (for secondary students) or 17 (for primary students) and then multiplying by 100 for an overall percentage.

The next step is for staff to develop improvement goals for the school discipline program. When conducting a school discipline assessment, you may find disagreement among groups regarding areas of strength and weakness. When this happens, you may need to go further by either running a second survey with deeper questions about the areas in dispute or by interviewing parents, staff members, and students for clarification on the thoughts behind their answers.

Interviews

The sample interview questions in Figure 2.9 can be used with a random group of staff members after the survey process has been completed. In this example, staff member surveys revealed low scores in the "relationship" category—a result at odds with the student and parent surveys, which scored statements in the same category as acceptable.

FIGURE 2.8
Buildingwide Discipline Assessment: Primary Students

Directions: Circle the happy face if you think the statement is true and the sad face if you think the statement is false.

1. I like our school.	😊 😠
2. I am rewarded for doing well.	😊 😠
3. I am proud when I do well.	😊 😠
4. I know the school rules.	😊 😠
5. My parents know the school rules.	😊 😠
6. If I get in trouble, the school calls my parents.	😊 😠
7. Students are nice to each other at my school.	😊 😠
8. My teachers treat me well.	😊 😠
9. If I get in trouble, my teachers treat me with respect.	😊 😠
10. I know what behaviors will get me sent to the office.	😊 😠
11. Teachers watch students in the halls.	😊 😠
12. Students behave well during assemblies.	😊 😠
13. Students behave well during lunch.	😊 😠
14. Students behave well during recess.	😊 😠
15. Students behave well in the halls.	😊 😠
16. Students are almost always on time to class.	😊 😠
17. Most of the students in our school do not bully other students.	😊 😠

FIGURE 2.9
Sample Staff Survey Comments and Interview Questions

Sample Staff Comments on School Discipline Assessment Surveys

• We have one recognition program, but that's not enough.

• We do recognition for sports but not for academics or citizenship.

• We don't involve parents in the sports recognition assemblies.

• Our students are very disrespectful.

• Some staff members are very disrespectful to others and even bully other staff members.

• It appears that some staff members are disrespectful and condescending when giving consequences to students.

Sample Staff Interview Questions Based on Comments

• What types of student recognition programs do you think the school should have?

• How do you think parents should be involved in recognition assemblies?

• Do you believe students are disrespectful to each other and to staff members? If so, describe the specific behaviors they display that are disrespectful.

• Do you believe some staff members are disrespectful and condescending when they give students consequences? If so, how?

• Do you believe some staff members are disrespectful to other staff members? If so, how many? What disrespectful behaviors do they display, and under what circumstances?

Direct Observations

To gather even more information about perceptions of the school discipline program, consider conducting direct observations. Although the most objective way to do this would be to use someone from outside the school with no preconceived notion regarding the effectiveness of the school's discipline program, this approach is often not feasible. The goal of the direct observation is to obtain objective data regarding the areas of concern noted on the surveys. The information collected must be specific and objective for the observations to be successful. Figure 2.10 shows an example of a completed observation form, including the observer's comments. Note that these comments are both specific and objective.

In the following chapters, we propose classroom and building action plans for each of our components of discipline.

FIGURE 2.10

Sample Observation Form

School: #15   **Date:** 4-13-07
Time Started: 8 a.m.   **Time Ended:** 3:30 p.m.

Look-Fors	Indicators
Morning before school	Three staff members on duty in front of the building as buses arrived; all students off buses in orderly fashion; all but five students to designated area at back of the building; three staff members on duty at back of the building
Tardies	Three students in halls after bell rang in the morning; no response from teachers as students entered classrooms
Hallways	Students well-behaved in hallways except for two who were pushing and shoving; two or three students in halls during classes with no hall passes; no staff members visible in hallways before or between classes; two areas of the building can't be seen from main hallway
Visible pride indicators	Some litter in the halls; student work displayed outside of 2 of 20 classrooms; state test results posted; athletic trophies in main hall
Lunchroom	Lunchroom rules posted; three staff members supervising students; students walk in and sit down and wait to be dismissed to line up for lunch; 12 students clean tables at the end of lunch; all students wait to be dismissed; students dismissed by table when all students quiet and table cleaned; lunchroom filled with litter after students leave
Lunch detention	80% of students assigned to detention arrive; 70% of students arrive late to detention; 30% of students in detention talking during detention; review of data shows 70% of students in detention are repeat offenders
Office referrals	About five students in the office per hour waiting to see principal; students waiting in office an average of 30 minutes to see administrator; all students talk while waiting in the office; review of office referral data shows students sent to office for talk outs and chewing gum
Recess and intramurals	Recess: Two supervisors for 500 students; boundaries of field large, one area of field not covered by or visible to supervisors; supervisors standing together and visiting; three student fights observed without intervention Intramurals: Two supervisors for 60 students; students playing basketball appropriately; all students responding appropriately to staff directives
Student respect	Eight students loudly swearing at each other; seven students in hallways refusing a staff member's directive to stop blocking the hall; six students pushing other students; 10 students running in the halls
After school	Ten students running in the halls; no supervisors at buses; five students running in front of the building before boarding buses

CHAPTER THREE

Action Plans for Relationships

After collecting data to assess the current state of the school discipline program, the discipline committee must determine what needs to happen to close the gap between the reality and the vision. The systemic action plan that the committee implements should embrace both collective autonomy and collective accountability.

Classroom Action Plan for Relationships

Tom has completed a self-assessment and has issues related to building positive relationships. His strengths are in the areas of parameters, monitoring, and consequences; his weaknesses are clearly in the relationship area for staff, parents, and students. His overall relationships score was 37 percent, with a parent relationships score of 60 percent, a staff relationships score of 20 percent, and a student relationships score of 30 percent.

A reflective teacher, working alone or with the principal, would quickly see that Tom needs to set goals in the area of developing positive relationships with parents, coworkers, and students. Before he can develop this plan, however, he needs some additional information. Following are some steps he can take to do this.

Step 1. Identify specific areas needing improvement. Tom should list all the statements on the relationships self-assessment survey for which the score was five or below. In his case, they are as follows:

Low staff relationships scores:
- I participate in all efforts to establish and maintain an effective school discipline program.
- I actively and consistently support school policies.
- When my students have discipline problems, I work collaboratively with colleagues to resolve the issues and develop plans.
- When working in groups, I keep an open mind and consider the needs of everyone.
- I am flexible and willing to make adjustments in my schedule and program if it meets the needs of colleagues or the school as a whole.

Low parent relationships scores:
- I proactively contact the parents of all my students to share positive information with them.
- I share my classroom rules with all of my students' parents at the beginning of the school year and follow up as needed.
- I let parents know when their children have done well or are being recognized.
- When meeting with parents, I begin each conference by saying something positive about the student.

Low student relationships scores:
- I do a good job of fostering student pride.
- I form strong, positive relationships with all of my students.
- I take a personal interest in all of my students.
- I welcome students as they enter my classroom each day.
- When giving students consequences, I always let them keep their dignity.
- I hold no grudges when students break rules.
- I communicate positive expectations to all of my students.
- Overall, my students treat each other with respect.
- Overall, my students treat staff members with respect.

Step 2. Write specific, measurable objectives for each of the areas needing improvement. When taking this step, teachers who don't have a repertoire of strategies to improve relationships may need additional help from books, from the principal, or from fellow teachers who already demonstrate strength in relationships. Lencioni (2002) suggests following these steps when consulting fellow staff members: admitting weaknesses and mistakes, asking for help, accepting questions and input about areas of responsibility, appreciating and tapping into one another's skills and experiences, and focusing on collective results by subjugating personal goals or interests for the good of the team.

Step 3. Develop the action plan, including data to collect to indicate progress. Figure 3.1 shows a sample action plan Tom could write to improve relationships with coworkers, students, and parents. It includes the three main goals he will work on, the specific action steps he will follow to achieve each goal, and the type of data he will collect to monitor his progress on the goals. The plan also includes a time line for each of the activities.

Step 4. Analyze the data and make adjustments to the plan. It isn't enough that Tom now has a plan in place to improve his relationships with students and staff members. He also needs to monitor himself as he implements the plan. The best way for him to do this is by reviewing the data from the plan daily and making an honest reflective assessment of how he is doing on each item. The dates in the plan are cues for Tom indicating when he should monitor each step.

According to his action plan, Tom will keep a diary that he should write in daily or weekly, indicating the date and making notes regarding each activity. As Covey (2004) notes, the practice of putting things in writing can help us learn from our failures and turn them into successes. To simplify his recordkeeping, Tom will indicate each activity by number (e.g., "1.1" to indicate goal 1, activity 1) rather than writing everything out. He should also make notes regarding what has been done to date. (See Figure 3.2 for an example of what an entry in Tom's log might look like.)

In the sample action plan, Tom indicates that he will keep a roster. This is basically a class list, labeled according to goal and activity. Tom should indicate the date each time he hands out a certificate and specify what type of certificate it is. (See Figure 3.3 for an example of what an entry in Tom's roster might look like.)

After reviewing and analyzing the data spelled out in his action plan, Tom should make adjustments as needed. We recommend doing so once every three months, but in some situations it may be appropriate to do so more or less frequently. For instance, goal 2.2 of Tom's action plan— "praise the class on a daily basis for specific, targeted behaviors"—may change from daily to biweekly or weekly praise when the reinforced behaviors become more automatic and part of the classroom culture.

As another example, when Tom reviews his notes in the log related to goal 1.4 ("Actively listen to others during discipline planning meetings, being careful to hold my opinion until all sides of the situation are voiced"), he may see statements such as, "January 5: I interrupted committee members three times during the meeting today to give my opinion" or "January 8: I didn't wait to hear all viewpoints before stating my own." An honest reflection of these notes would make it clear to Tom that he needs coaching or training in active listening. This being the case, a new objective might be, "Take a class in active listening and practice techniques learned in the class during discipline committee meetings." Realistically, this level of self-honesty and self-reflection requires a highly mature and skilled individual, which is rare. It may be that the principal needs to monitor and analyze the data to help with adjusting the objectives for the teacher.

School Action Plan for Relationships

Now consider a school that has strong scores for parameters (80 percent), monitoring (70 percent), and consequences (90 percent), but has a low relationships score of 40 percent. Data from the staff member surveys indicate that the specific areas of concern with relationships are staff-to-student, staff-to-staff, staff-to-parent, student-to-staff, and student-to-student. Some typical staff member comments on surveys include the following:

- "Students are disrespectful to each other and to staff members."
- "Staff members are disrespectful to each other, and some staff members openly bully others."
- "Staff members are not welcoming to parents or community members."

Scores and comments on the parent surveys confirm these concerns, with parents expressing a low comfort level when contacting

FIGURE 3.1
Sample Teacher Action Plan: Relationships

Goals	Action Steps	Evaluation Data	When
1. Improve relationships with staff members	1. Provide constructive input in the discipline planning process at meetings, on surveys, etc.	Log	When they occur
	2. Actively and consistently follow the agreed-upon buildingwide discipline policy	Log	Daily
	3. Work collaboratively with other staff members to develop and implement individual student discipline plans	Log	As needed
	4. Actively listen to others during discipline planning meetings, being careful to hold my opinion until all sides of the situation are voiced	Log	At meetings
	5. Whenever possible, adjust my schedule to help meet the needs of team members	Log	As needed
2. Improve relationships with students	1. Give a citizenship certificate to students at least every three months for specific, positive behaviors	Student roster	Citizenship assemblies
	2. Praise the class on a daily basis for specific, targeted behaviors (e.g., lining up quietly, walking quietly in the halls, complying quickly with my signal)	Log	Daily
	3. Use courtesy when giving students instructions, corrections, and directives	Log	Daily
	4. Learn personal interests of all students in the classroom and make positive individual comments to students regarding their interests throughout the year	Student roster	Daily
	5. Greet students at the classroom door with a smile/handshake at least three times a week	Log	Three times a week
	6. When correcting students' behaviors, do so in a private, positive way, allowing them to keep their dignity	Log	Daily
	7. When disciplining students, let them know that I know they can do better in the future	Log	Daily
	8. Model respectful language and behaviors for students	Log	Daily
	9. Teach students a rubric for respectful behavior toward staff and peers	Log	By Sept. 15

FIGURE 3.1—*continued*
Sample Teacher Action Plan: Relationships

Goals	Action Steps	Evaluation Data	When
	10. Give students specific, positive feedback regarding their respectful behaviors and give appropriate consequences for disrespectful behaviors	Log	Daily
3. Improve relationships with parents	1. Make positive phone calls to all students' parents	Log	One contact per parent quarterly
	2. Communicate classroom rules to parents in writing and verbally	Copy of letter, open house agenda	Letter sent by Sept. 15, open house by Sept. 15
	3. Invite parents to citizenship assemblies when their students are being recognized	Phone call log	One week before assembly
	4. Begin each meeting with a parent by saying something positive about their student	Log	All parent conferences

school staff members or visiting the school. The student surveys also have low scores in the areas related to relationships, suggesting a low level of respect among students for their peers and teachers and excessive bullying behaviors. Many of the surveys also indicate that students don't believe their teachers care about them, and that there are not enough adequate recognition assemblies at the school. After reviewing all of the information from the surveys, the school discipline committee should take the following steps to develop an action plan to improve relationships.

FIGURE 3.2
Sample Log Entry

Date	Goal	Data
Feb. 1	1.1	I made recommendations for improvement for lunch detention during a staff meeting.

FIGURE 3.3
Sample Roster Entry

Goal 2.1: Citizenship Certificates

Student	Date	Type of Certificate
Stan Johnson	3-1-06	Certificate for respectful behavior

Step 1. Identify specific areas needing improvement. The discipline committee should first examine those survey statements that received low scores. The specific items of low relationships scores from the surveys for our sample school are as follows:

- Our school has effective programs and strategies to develop student pride buildingwide.
- Our school maintains an effective buildingwide focus on recognizing student achievement.
- Our school does an effective job of letting parents know when students have done well or are being recognized.
- Overall, our students treat each other with respect.
- Overall, our students treat staff members with respect.
- Overall, staff members treat each other with respect.

Additional information can be gathered in the form of interviews or observations with staff members and students. Figure 3.4 shows what an interview form could look like for our sample school. Figure 3.5 shows what an observation form might look like for our sample school. Observations can be made over a week rather than in a single day.

In examining the data on the interview and observation forms, the discipline committee at the sample school decided that the information needed to be shared with administration, as some of the behaviors they noted constituted evaluation issues. In sharing the data, they also provided the names of the specific teachers observed.

Step 2. Write specific, measurable objectives for each of the identified goal areas.

Step 3. Develop the action plan, including data to collect to indicate progress. Figure 3.6 shows what an action plan developed by the discipline committee at our sample school might look like.

FIGURE 3.4

Sample Staff Interview Form for
School Action Plan: Relationships

Date: _____   Certificated or Classified Staff Member? _____

Please supply your comments about any of the following issues.

Staff-to-Student Relationships

Some staff members talk disrespectfully to students and don't treat them with dignity.

_____

_____

_____

Some staff members enjoy giving students consequences.

_____

_____

_____

Some staff members are poor models of respectful behaviors.

_____

_____

_____

Staff-to-Staff Relationships

Some staff members are disrespectful to coworkers.

_____

_____

_____

Some staff members make derogatory remarks about coworkers.

_____

_____

_____

Some staff members make faces and roll their eyes when coworkers make comments with which they don't agree.

_____

_____

_____

FIGURE 3.4—*continued*
Sample Staff Interview Form for
School Action Plan: Relationships

Student-to-Student Relationships

Some students bully other students.

_____

_____

_____

Some students use inappropriate language with each other.

_____

_____

_____

Some students threaten harm to other students.

_____

_____

_____

Student-to-Staff Relationships

Some students are disrespectful to staff members.

_____

_____

_____

Staff-to-Parent Relationships

Some staff members are unfriendly to parents.

_____

_____

_____

Some staff members are not welcoming or helpful to parents.

_____

_____

_____

FIGURE 3.5
Sample Staff Observation Form
for School Action Plan: Relationships

Date: 4-9-07 to 4-13-07

Look-Fors	Observer Comments
Staff to Student	Three staff members observed yelling at students on three separate occasions
Staff to Staff	Three staff members observed gossiping about other staff members on two occasions; three staff members observed laughing inappropriately at coworker comments at staff meeting
Student to Student	Many students observed bullying other students in the halls throughout the week
Student to Staff	Ten students observed using inappropriate language with staff members
Staff to Parents	Five comments by parents complaining about three staff members being rude to them

Step 4. Analyze the data and make adjustments to the plan. Monitoring meeting minutes and lesson plans would be the best way for administrators at our sample school to ensure that the activities in the action plan are accomplished. Simply writing the plan or communicating the goals is not enough. Also, the results should be analyzed and adjusted as needed on at least a quarterly basis. For example, Goals 4.1 and 5.1 in Figure 3.6—"All teachers teach students the Respect Rubric"—may need to be repeated if significant numbers of students continue to be disrespectful. An additional step would be to have an administrator or intervention specialist work with smaller groups of students identified as regularly disrespectful.

The end result of implementing and monitoring the action plan should be improvement in relationships throughout the school, a more positive school climate, and greater general discipline. One way of assessing the action plan's success is to have staff members, parents, and students retake the initial surveys, and compare the "before and after" results.

FIGURE 3.6
Sample School Action Plan: Relationships

Goals	Action Steps	Evaluation Data	When
1. Improve staff-to-student relationships	1. Administration provides a workshop for staff in which strategies for developing positive student relationships are reviewed	Meeting minutes	By Sept. 30
	2. Discipline committee members form a subcommittee to develop one student recognition program for each building-wide consequence	Committee meeting minutes	Within one month
	3. Recognition subcommittee identifies at least three new areas of school pride to focus on with an implementation plan	Subcommittee meeting minutes	Within one month
2. Improve staff-to-staff relationships	1. Discipline committee identifies specific negative behaviors demonstrated by some staff members through an anonymous survey	Survey results	By Oct. 30
	2. Discipline committee and administration share the results of the staff survey with all staff	Meeting minutes	By Dec. 10
	3. Administration shares expectations for appropriate staff behaviors with all staff, as well as what disciplinary or evaluation steps will be taken for staff who display inappropriate behaviors in the future	Contract and meeting minutes	By Dec. 10
	4. Administration hires a consultant to work with staff members on how to effectively and proactively deal with inappropriate staff behaviors	Meeting minutes	By Jan. 30
	5. Administration deals appropriately with staff members who continue to display negative behaviors	Staff evaluations	Ongoing
3. Improve staff-to-parent relationships	1. Administration covers each teacher's class for 30 minutes so that teacher can make positive phone calls to parents concerning their student's behaviors	Administrator's schedule	Once per semester
	2. Administration holds a discussion at two staff meetings soliciting strategies for making parents feel welcome in the school	Meeting minutes	By Nov. 30
	3. All teachers write a goal for improving parent relationships in their annual goals	Staff goals	By Oct. 15

FIGURE 3.6—*continued*
Sample School Action Plan: Relationships

Goals	Action Steps	Evaluation Data	When
	4. Administration deals individually with staff members identified in parent complaints	Administrative notes; staff discipline records	As needed
4. Improve student-to-student relationships	1. All teachers teach students the Respect Rubric (see Chapter 4, p. 52)	Lesson plans	By Oct. 1
	2. Staff members implement consequences as stipulated in the buildingwide rules when students are disrespectful as defined in the Respect Rubric	Discipline records	As needed
	3. Staff members teach students what bullying behaviors are and what the consequences will be for displaying these behaviors	Staff meeting minutes and lesson plans	By Sept. 30
	4. Staff members implement consequences as stipulated in the building-wide rules when students bully one another	Discipline records	As needed
5. Improve student-to-staff relationships	1. All teachers teach students the Respect Rubric (see Chapter 4, p. 52)	Lesson plans	By Oct. 1
	2. Staff members implement consequences as stipulated in the buildingwide rules when students are disrespectful as defined in the Respect Rubric	Discipline records	As needed

Possible Challenges

The biggest challenge with the sample bulding action plan, as with all action plans, lies in monitoring the implementation cycle. If this is not done, the chances of the plan being completed are very low. This is why a person or group should be assigned to each of the action steps. In addition, someone should be assigned to monitor implementation of the overall plan. This is very often, but not always, the administration. If it is not the administration, it should be the school discipline committee.

In our experience working with schools throughout the United States, we have found that it is often more effective for the discipline committee to conduct the monitoring. Administrative turnover can be very high, and new administrators may not share the vision of high-level discipline. Unfortunately, we have seen several examples of schools with weak administration. Ideally, monitoring should be a joint effort between the discipline committee and the administration, with administrators taking the lead but with the discipline committee holding onto the vision.

Monitoring can also be a challenge when there are staff members who contribute to a negative climate. We have seen schools where some staff members bully their coworkers. Such situations need to be dealt with very carefully, with the support and guidance of the district office and of the teachers union.

Staff members need to have the courage to voice their concerns, specifically identify the inappropriate behaviors of staff members, deal appropriately with the offending individual themselves, and report the behaviors as necessary. It is always best if a staff member can first deal with an offending coworker on his or her own. When this approach is not effective, however, it is important that he or she take the next step and report the offense to the administration, which must then take whatever disciplinary or evaluative steps are necessary.

CHAPTER FOUR

Action Plans for Parameters

Classroom Action Plan for Parameters

Sue, a 3rd grade teacher, has a decent overall discipline score on her self-assessment survey, but is weak in the area of setting clearly defined parameters of acceptable student behaviors. The action plan for Sue will look very different from the one for Tom in Chapter 3. Following are some steps Sue can take to create a successful action plan for addressing her parameters issues.

Step 1. Identify when student behaviors are problematic. Assuming that Sue's classroom schedule is fairly consistent from day to day, she should first identify the times of day when student behaviors are problematic.

Example: Sue identifies the following three times of day: when students first enter her classroom in the morning, when they are involved in classroom discussions, and when they leave her classroom.

Step 2. Identify negative behaviors and desired behaviors. Sue should identify what specific inappropriate behaviors students display in her class during the times identified in step 1, and what behaviors she wants them to demonstrate instead.

Example: Sue notes that when students first enter the classroom, they are loud and boisterous. About half of them are still getting drinks and sharpening their pencils after the bell has rung, and about a third of them are talking when they should be working on the daily activity posted on the overhead. What she would like students to do instead is enter the classroom quietly, put their coats away immediately, sharpen their pencils, get their drinks, and be sitting down working by the time the bell rings. During classroom discussions, Sue notes, students blurt out answers, leave their seats, sharpen pencils, and get drinks. She would prefer that all students raise their hands to speak, remain seated, and pay attention to the speaker during discussions. When students leave Sue's class, she notes that they line up noisily, leave messes on their desks, and push one another. Sue would like the students to line up quickly and quietly when she calls their rows, keep their desks cleared off, remain silent in line, stay on the right side of the hallway, and keep their hands to themselves.

Step 3. Teach the rules of conduct and the rationale for each. Sue should teach her rules of conduct for entering the classroom, classroom discussions, and transitioning to other classrooms. She has already clearly identified desired behaviors in step 2, and now needs to explain to students why these behaviors are important. She should also teach the expected behaviors, and require that students practice them until mastery.

Example: Sue could begin a lesson on appropriate behaviors when entering the classroom by saying the following: "Class, I've noticed that we're wasting a lot of learning time first thing in the morning because people are visiting with each other and sharpening pencils instead of working on the overhead activity. It's important that we get right to work because we have so many things to cover each day, and if we're not careful we'll run out of time. On the wall, I've posted a list of what I expect you to do when you enter the classroom every morning and what I want to see happen before the bell rings."

Sue's list reads as follows:

1. Hang up your coats.
2. Sharpen your pencils and get your drinks.
3. Turn in your homework.
4. Go to your desks and silently work on the overhead activity.
5. Be in your seat working when the bell rings.

After reviewing the list and answering questions, Sue should direct the class to practice the procedures. She can do this by taking the students into the hall and having them reenact entering the classroom. Afterward, she should give them specific feedback on their performance every day for a week. After a week, the behaviors should be established. However, if Sue sees that students are lapsing, she should reteach the rules of conduct. (Another way for Sue to verify that students understand the expected behaviors is to give them a written test that requires them to answer specific questions about the expected behaviors.)

Step 4. Develop the action plan, including data to collect to indicate progress. Figure 4.1 shows an action plan Sue could write to better set parameters of acceptable student behavior. The plan includes her overall goal, what she plans to do to accomplish the goal, and what data she will collect to show that she has completed each activity.

The process described above can be followed for any grade level and for any rules of conduct. Ideally, teachers should teach all rules of conduct at the beginning of the year so students know what the expectations are, but even in the best of situations, certain times of the day breed more problematic behaviors than others. (If a teacher is not particularly reflective, administrators may step in to help him or her identify behavioral problems and what needs to be done about them.)

School Action Plan for Parameters

Now consider a school that has acceptable scores in all areas except for parameters, where it scores 40 percent overall (and less than 4 on all parameters-related areas). As in Sue's case, more information must be gathered to put together an effective action plan. The discipline committee should take the following steps to address the school's parameters issues.

Step 1. Identify the specific problem areas in the building.

Step 2. Identify negative behaviors and desired behaviors. For both steps 1 and 2, the school discipline committee should examine the statements on the initial surveys that deal with locations. For example, in the monitoring section of the staff survey (see page 18), there are questions

FIGURE 4.1

Sample Teacher Action Plan: Parameters

Goal	Action Steps	Evaluation Data	When
1. Set clearly defined parameters of acceptable student behaviors	1. Identify when student behaviors are problematic	Log	Ongoing
	2. Identify negative and desired behaviors for entering the classroom, classroom discussions, and leaving the classroom	List of negative behaviors and list of desired behaviors	First week of school
	3. Teach rules of conduct and rationales for entering the classroom, classroom discussions, and leaving the classroom	Lesson plan	First week of school
	4. Post the rules of conduct for entering the classroom, classroom discussions, and leaving the classroom	Posted rules	First day of school
	5. Have students practice appropriate conduct until mastery	Lesson plan	First week of school
	6. Reteach the rules of conduct whenever necessary	Lesson plan	When necessary
	7. Administer a test to students on rules of conduct	Lesson plan, copy of test, test results	Second week of school

about lunchrooms, assemblies, and hallways, and there are similar questions in the student and parent surveys. A follow-up staff survey such as the one in Figure 4.2 can provide additional information regarding specific inappropriate behaviors. These survey results should be supplemented by direct observations in the identified locations. (Keep in mind that when making direct observations, the presence of an observer can skew the data somewhat.)

Let's assume that a school discipline committee identifies hallways, the lunchroom, and the stairs from the lunchroom to the hallway as areas of concern on the follow-up staff survey. For the hallways, negative behaviors include running, tardiness, and inappropriate language; for the lunchroom, negative behaviors include throwing food, pushing in line, and leaving tables messy; and for the stairs, negative behaviors include running, pushing and shoving, and walking three to four abreast (as opposed to single file).

FIGURE 4.2
Sample Follow-Up Staff Survey: Parameters

Directions: Please identify which of the following building locations are areas of concern when it comes to student behaviors. For each location identified, please specify the negative behaviors observed (e.g., running, shouting, inappropriate language).

○ Hallways

○ Playground during recess

○ Lunchroom

○ Gymnasium during assemblies

○ Gymnasium during intramurals

○ Buses

○ Outdoor grounds before school

○ Outdoor grounds after school

○ Other

The school discipline committee might also conduct random interviews of about a quarter of the staff to gather additional data. Figure 4.3 shows an example of an interview form with sample staff comments.

In addition to the interviews, the school discipline committee can conduct direct observations of student behaviors using a form like the one in Figure 4.4.

FIGURE 4.3
Sample Follow-Up Staff Interview Form: Parameters

Date: 2-9-07

Certificated or Classified Staff Member? _____

Do you have any comments or concerns about any student behaviors in the following locations?

○ Hallways:

Students run and yell. _____

○ Lunchroom:

Students run, and some throw food. _____

○ Stairs:

Students run, shove, and push, and some crowd the stairs. _____

Step 3. Examine the school rules that address the locations identified, make certain each rule is worded clearly, and state consequences for rule violations. In our example, the school rules direct students to "use appropriate behaviors in the hallways and not linger after the bell rings," "display appropriate behaviors at all times in the lunchroom," and "walk appropriately up and down the stairs." In examining the rules, the school discipline committee finds none that address either respect for students and staff or tardiness.

The good news is that each of the identified "problem" locations is addressed in the rules. The bad news is that the parameters for acceptable student behaviors in each location are vague, and none of the rules address what consequences students can expect to receive for rule violations. This lack of explicitness leads to confusion regarding expectations and inconsistency of enforcement, and can eventually result in chaos.

Step 4. Revise rules as needed, making expectations and consequences specific and clear. Continuing with our example, the school discipline

FIGURE 4.4
**Sample Staff Observation Form
for School Action Plan: Parameters**

Date: 2-12-07 to 2-16-07

Look-Fors	Observer Comments
Hallways	Ten students observed tardy to class; four students observed running
Playground during recess	Students up to three minutes late responding to line-up whistle
Lunchroom	Three students observed throwing food; two students observed running
Gymnasium during assemblies	About 10 percent of teachers observed sitting with their students

committee revises the wording of each rule based on the specific negative behaviors that staff have identified. Their draft rewording of the rules reads as follows:

- Hallways: "Students should use appropriate language, keep their hands to themselves, and not linger in the hallways. Violations of these behaviors will result in lunch detention or after-school detention."
- Tardiness: "Unless they have a hall pass, students should be in their assigned classrooms after the bell rings. Repeated tardiness will result in lunch detention or after-school detention."
- Lunchroom: "Students should be escorted to the lunchroom by their teacher and remain seated at their assigned tables until directed to line up. Inappropriate language, throwing food, and pushing and shoving are not allowed. After eating, students should clean up their areas and take their trays to the designated area when directed to do so by staff. Students should line up and walk quietly to class at the direction of their teachers. Violation of any of these rules will result in an immediate lunch detention or after-school detention for severe or repeated violations."

- Stairs: "Students should walk single file on the right side of the stairs. Failure to do so will result in lunch detention."
- Respect: "Students should act respectfully toward everyone at all times. Failure to do so will result in lunch detention, after-school detention, Friday school, or (in extreme cases) suspension."

In this case, further explanation and definition for the terms "appropriate language" and "respect" are needed, and should be articulated next.

Step 5. Determine what rule violations warrant office referrals. For this process to work effectively, everyone at the school should be clear about what constitutes an office referral, and all staff should consistently follow the guidelines so that effective consequences can justifiably be applied. If staff members are sending students to the office for behaviors that they should be dealing with themselves, administration should deal with the staff members appropriately. Behaviors that should be referred to the office include physical threats, violence, blatant noncompliance, gang behaviors, and behaviors that seriously disrupt the educational process. Administrators should work closely with staff to identify the guidelines for making office referrals. Terms such as "physical threats," "violent behaviors," or "blatant noncompliance" should be clarified, so that everyone knows what they actually mean. The staff may need in-service training from the local police department regarding gang behaviors.

Step 6. Teach the rules to students and staff. Any time there are changes to school rules, they should be reviewed and taught to the students—preferably at the beginning of the year. Just passing out handbooks that include the rules or stating the rules is not sufficient. Remember, students do not learn what is simply announced; they learn what is taught.

Teachers should prepare a lesson that teaches each of the rules. The lesson should begin with a discussion of the rationale for each rule, followed by a guided discussion and student practice. For example, if a teacher is teaching the rules for lunchroom behavior, he or she may wish to take the students to the lunchroom, where they can practice walking appropriately in line, taking their seats immediately, waiting for the signal from the teacher to line up for lunch, returning to their tables, cleaning up their areas, waiting to be dismissed, returning their trays, and lining up again to return to their classroom. This "dress rehearsal" process dramatically increases the chances that students will heed the rules.

Students need to know what "inappropriate language" actually means. There are some words that everyone knows are inappropriate; these don't need to be defined. However, there are other words that students think are acceptable in school because they hear them at home or on the street. For example, students may not realize that the word "gay" is unacceptable when used as a synonym for "uncool," or that "What's up, ho?" is not an acceptable greeting. Students need to know that if they use such words in school, they will receive a consequence. They also need to know that any racial slurs are unacceptable, even when used among students of the same race.

"Respect" is another word that often needs to be taught. Students need to be clear about what it means to respect others. As with certain words, what students may consider respectful at home or on the street may not be acceptable at school. In clarifying the meaning of respect, there are two useful approaches. One is to simply list respectful behaviors (e.g., "use appropriate language, keep your hands to yourselves, comply with all staff directives on first request"); the other is to design a rubric that includes various levels of such behaviors (see Figure 4.5).

Alternatively, Charlotte Danielson (1996) suggests the following four levels of respect:

1. Student interactions are characterized by conflict, sarcasm, or put-downs.
2. Students do not demonstrate negative behavior toward one another.
3. Student interactions are generally polite and respectful.
4. Students demonstrate genuine caring for one another as individuals and as students. (p. 80)

Administrators should visit every classroom in the school to share the most recent school rules and review the rationale and consequences for each. When students hear the rules from administrators as well as from their teachers, they can appreciate that the rules have unanimous support. Rules can also be taught at assemblies, perhaps through skits in which students role-play positive and negative examples of the rules.

Step 7. Communicate the rules to parents. The best way to communicate the school rules to parents is in writing. Schools should require parents to sign a statement saying that they have read and will support the school rules, and then keep these signed statements on file. Open houses, back-to-school nights, and parent conferences are excellent opportunities to explain any new rules to parents.

FIGURE 4.5
Rubric of Respectful Behaviors

4 Exemplary	3 Competent	2 Emerging	1 Unacceptable
The student	The student	The student	The student
• Never uses inappropriate or derogatory language.	• Never uses inappropriate or derogatory language.	• Rarely uses inappropriate or derogatory language.	• Uses inappropriate or derogatory language.
• Always says "please" and "thank you" when requesting or receiving.	• Often says "please" and "thank you" when requesting or receiving.	• Sometimes says "please" and "thank you" when requesting or receiving.	• Never says "please" and "thank you."
• Always keeps hands to himself or herself.	• Always keeps hands to himself or herself.	• Often keeps hands to himself or herself.	• Does not keep hands to himself or herself.
• Always complies with staff directives on the first request.	• Usually complies with staff directives on the first request.	• Usually complies with staff directives on the first request.	• Does not comply with staff directives on the first request.

Step 8. Post the rules. Posted rules serve as a reminder to students, staff members, and parents. The rules should be posted prominently in relevant places (e.g., lunchroom rules in the lunchroom, hallway rules in the hallways) and by classroom doors, where they can serve as daily reminders for teachers and students alike.

Step 9. Reteach the rules following long school breaks or whenever students appear to need reminders. Certain rules are more frequently violated at particular times of the year; rules against sexual harassment, for example, are more often violated in the spring, when students wear more revealing clothes. Principals may wish to visit classrooms at these times to reteach the rules and attendant consequences.

Step 10. Develop an action plan. Figure 4.6 shows an action plan that the school in our example might write to improve its performance regarding parameters. After developing and implementing the buildingwide action

FIGURE 4.6

Sample School Action Plan: Parameters

Goals	Action Steps	Evaluation Data	When
1. Set clearly defined parameters of acceptable student behaviors	1. Staff members identify the specific problem areas in the building	List of locations	By Sept. 1
	2. Staff members identify negative behaviors and desired behaviors in the problem areas	List of behaviors	By Sept. 1
	3. Staff members examine the school rules that address the problem areas, making certain each rule is worded clearly and stating consequences for rule violations	List of rules	By Sept. 1
	4. Staff members revise rules as needed, making expectations and consequences specific and clear	Revised rules	By Sept. 1
	5. Staff members determine what rule violations warrant office referrals	List of rules	By Sept. 1
	6. Administrators teach the rules to students and staff	Meeting minutes	By Sept. 1
	7. Administrators communicate the rules to parents	Parent letter	By Sept. 1
	8. Staff members post the rules	Posted rules	Ongoing
	9. Staff members reteach the rules following long school breaks or whenever students appear to need reminders	Meeting minutes	Ongoing

plan, the school discipline committee should readminister the parameters survey.

Possible Challenges

One of the biggest challenges we have seen in our work with schools throughout the United States is inconsistent implementation of all rules at all times. Individual staff members often choose to ignore rules that they don't truly support. For example, let's say a school prohibits students from bringing backpacks to class, for safety reasons. Some teachers at the school disagree that backpacks are safety hazards, so they simply look the other way when students break the rule. It quickly becomes clear to students that these teachers will let students get away with breaking the rules.

When teachers flout school rules, they negatively affect the school climate. Administrators must therefore ensure that teachers enforce school policies whether they agree with them or not, and deal appropriately with teachers who refuse.

CHAPTER FIVE

Action Plans for Monitoring

Classroom Action Plan for Monitoring

John, a 7th grade teacher, has a low overall monitoring score of 30 percent. Following are some steps John can take to create an action plan that address his monitoring issues.

Step 1. Identify specific low-scoring areas. John notes that he scored below 5 on the following items:

- I consistently and effectively use monitoring skills in my classroom with all of my students.
- I am visible in the halls during transition periods.
- I monitor my students' behaviors in assemblies.
- I move around the room during teacher-led instruction and independent seatwork.
- During teacher-led instruction, I do not hesitate to use monitoring skills when I see that a student is off task or behaving inappropriately.

Step 2. Write specific, measurable objectives for each of the identified areas. After identifying the specific areas needing attention, John should determine strategies to improve each of them. Because he is not sure of the proximity patterns he typically uses during instruction or independent seatwork, he asks a colleague to observe him at work, and to return one month later to gauge any improvement in performance. One of the most powerful ways to increase self-awareness is to seek input from others. As Covey (2004) notes, feedback from people who are successful in a particular area can bring clarity to our blind spots and accelerate our personal growth.

Step 3. Develop an action plan including data that indicates progress. Based on John's review of his low scores and input from peers and his principal, he drafts the action plan in Figure 5.1 to improve his monitoring skills.

FIGURE 5.1
Sample Teacher Action Plan: Monitoring

Goal	Action Steps	Evaluation Data	When
1. Improve monitoring skills	1. Have a colleague conduct two 20-minute observations and record use of response opportunities, latency, and proximity during teacher-led instruction	Response Opportunity Chart, Latency Chart, Proximity Chart	By Nov. 1
	2. Have a colleague conduct two 20-minute observations and record use of teacher-student interactions and proximity during independent seatwork	Teacher-Student Interaction Chart, Proximity Chart	By Dec. 1
	3. Based on data from observations in steps 1.1 and 1.2, create a new action plan to specifically improve monitoring patterns	New action plan	By Jan. 15
	4. Have a colleague repeat steps 1.1 and 1.2	Charts in steps 1.1 and 1.2	By May 1
	5. Stand in the hallways during transition periods	Log	Three days a week
	6. Sit next to and monitor students during assemblies	Log	All assemblies
	7. Consistently and appropriately follow through with students who are tardy	Discipline referrals	Daily

When observing John's monitoring patterns, John's colleague uses

- A Response Opportunity Chart (Figure 5.2) to note whenever John provides a student with a response opportunity (that is, whenever he calls on a student or asks a question);
- A Latency Chart (Figure 5.3) to record the amount of time the teacher gives a student to respond after being called on or being asked a question; and
- A Proximity Chart (Figure 5.4) to note John's movement around the room. (In this particular example, "X" indicates a stop of at least 2 seconds. Also, because John moves around so much, the observer has broken the chart down into four charts, each representing one 5-minute period.)

Teachers may also wish to use computer software to keep track of monitoring behaviors. Such software can be used to track class learning time, attention to gender, nonverbal behaviors, and student responses.

Step 4. Analyze the observation data and make adjustments in the plan. John's Proximity Chart shows that he is neglecting to consistently use proximity with the center two rows of students. To address this situation, he may wish to add the following goal to his action plan: "Focus on consistently walking past all students in the classroom."

If John implements his action plan and monitors his progress, there's no question that he will improve his monitoring skills, resulting in a decreased need for consequences. To confirm the success of his plan, John might analyze his discipline referrals before and after implementation and retake the self-assessment survey.

School Action Plan for Monitoring

Now consider a school that has high relationships, parameters, and consequences scores, but a monitoring score of 30 percent. On their surveys, parents and students commented that teachers were oblivious to bullying and often hard to find in the hallways. Staff surveys confirmed the latter observation.

Here are some steps that this school can use to address monitoring issues.

Step 1. Identify specific low-scoring areas. The discipline committee at our sample school found that the following items received scores of 5 or less on staff surveys:

- Administrators maintain a high level of visibility buildingwide throughout the day.
- All staff members actively support the school rules.
- Staff members monitor student behavior during assemblies.
- Staff members monitor student behavior during lunch.
- Staff members monitor student behavior during recess and intramural events.
- Staff members monitor student behavior in the hallways.
- Staff members monitor student behavior before and after school.

FIGURE 5.2
Sample Response Opportunity Chart

Sara ✓	Kaitlyn	Bob	Jamie
Joe	Katie	Mark ✓✓	Janice ✓
Tom ✓✓✓	Carrie ✓✓✓	Kelley	Randi
Fred	Ryan	Tyler ✓✓✓✓	Dominique
Karl	Beth	Brianne	Lester

Step 2. Write specific, measurable objectives for each of the problem areas identified. The discipline committee at our sample school conducted staff interviews and direct observations buildingwide before developing specific objectives (see Figures 5.5 and 5.6 for examples of the interview and observation forms used).

Step 3. Develop an action plan. Based on the specific information gathered from surveys, interviews, and direct observations, the discipline committee brainstormed action steps and supporting data for each of the identified goal areas (see Figure 5.7 for a sample building action plan for monitoring behaviors).

FIGURE 5.3
Sample Latency Chart

Sara 2″	Kaitlyn	Bob	Jamie
Joe	Katie	Mark 5″, 7″	Janice 2″
Tom 3″, 5″, 7″	Carrie 3″	Kelley	Randi
Fred	Ryan	Tyler 3″, 3″, 5″, 7″	Dominique
Karl	Beth	Brianne	Lester

The conflict managers program referred to in goal 5.2 of the action plan trains intermediate students to serve as mediators on the playground, reducing the number of problems that need to be referred to playground supervisors. One such program is the "All Stars" program at Minter Creek Elementary School in Gig Harbor, Washington, where select 5th grade students are trained to help resolve potential recess conflicts through peer mediation. These students must apply to participate in the program; if "hired," they are paid in coupons valid at the school store. The popularity of this program has created a culture of strong communication skills and creative problem solving at Minter Creek.

Step 4. Analyze the data and made adjustments in the plan. The school discipline committee must work with the administration to monitor the building action plan after it is implemented. We often hear teachers say that their principals need to monitor them to ensure that they're doing what they agreed to do.

Let's say that, in our sample school, several staff members consistently miss their assigned duties for goals 2–7. In such a case, administrators may wish to remind all staff about their duties through e-mails and staff meetings. If these reminders are not heeded, it is the administration's responsibility to follow through and discipline the offending staff members. Without administrative monitoring, teachers become disgruntled, students grow to believe that the rules are meaningless, and the culture of the school is at risk of becoming divisive. It takes a strong and courageous leader to hold everyone responsible in a caring yet direct manner.

FIGURE 5.4
Sample Proximity Chart

Front of Classroom

Sara X	Kaitlyn	Bob	Jamie
Joe	Katie	Mark	Janice X
Tom	Carrie	Kelley	Randi
Fred	Ryan	Tyler	Dominique
Karl	Beth	Brianne	Lester

10:00–10:05 a.m.

Front of Classroom

Sara	Kaitlyn	Bob X	Jamie
Joe	Katie	Mark	Janice
Tom	Carrie	Kelley	Randi
Fred	Ryan	Tyler	Dominique
Karl	Beth X	Brianne	Lester

10:05–10:10 a.m.

FIGURE 5.4—*continued*
Sample Proximity Chart

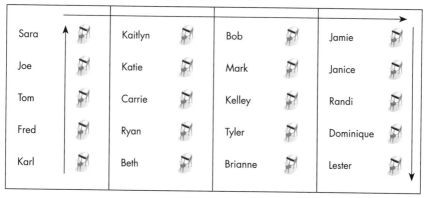

Front of Classroom

Sara	Kaitlyn	Bob	Jamie
Joe	Katie	Mark	Janice
Tom	Carrie	Kelley	Randi
Fred	Ryan	Tyler	Dominique
Karl	Beth	Brianne	Lester

10:10–10:15 a.m.

Front of Classroom

Sara	Kaitlyn	Bob	Jamie
Joe	Katie	Mark	Janice
Tom	Carrie	Kelley	Randi
Fred	Ryan	Tyler	Dominique
Karl	Beth	Brianne	Lester

10:15–10:20 a.m.

FIGURE 5.5
Sample Follow-Up Staff Interview Form: Monitoring

Date: 2-9-07

Certificated or Classified Staff Member? _____

Do you have any comments or concerns about any monitoring behaviors among staff in the following locations?

○ Hallways:

We rarely see administrators in the halls between classes; teachers remain in their classes during transition times.

○ Buses:

Administrators are never outside near the buses; sometimes teachers who have bus duty miss their assignments.

○ Gymnasium during assemblies:

Teachers sit together rather than with their classes.

○ Lunchroom:

Only one paraprofessional is on duty during lunch; students are loud and rowdy and throw food.

○ Outdoors during recess or intramural activities:

There is only one supervisor for approximately 400 students, and there are many blind spots.

Do you have any concerns regarding consistent implementation of buildingwide rules by staff?

Many staff member ignore the school rules; no one holds staff accountable; no one monitors staff behaviors.

FIGURE 5.6
Sample Staff Observation Form for School Action Plan: Monitoring

Date: 2-12-07 to 2-16-07

Look-Fors	Observer Comments
Hallways	No staff observed monitoring in halls during transition periods
Buses	Two of three assigned staff members on duty during bus drop-off and pick-up
Outdoors before and after school	About 10 students on grounds unsupervised before and after school
Outdoors during recess or intramural activities	One staff member on duty for approximately 400 students; several blind spots with students unsupervised
Lunchroom	Only one supervisor on duty; students are loud in line, run around, throw food, act disrespectfully
Gymnasium during assemblies	One teacher sat with her students, while the others sat together talking; students talked during assembly

FIGURE 5.7
Sample School Action Plan: Monitoring

Goals	Action Steps	Evaluation Data	When
1. Improve monitoring of student behaviors by administration	1. Administrators monitor the hallways during passing periods	Administrators' daily schedule	At least three times a week
	2. Administrators monitor the front of the building when buses arrive at least three times a week	Administrators' daily schedule	At least three times a week
2. Improve all staff support of agreed-upon building policies and rules.	1. Administrators monitor all staff for consistent implementation of discipline policies and rules	Administrator observations with teacher input	Ongoing
3. Improve all staff monitoring of student behaviors during assemblies	1. All teachers sit with their classes during assemblies	Administrator observations	All assemblies
4. Improve staff monitoring of student behaviors during lunch	1. Administration develops and implements a staff lunch supervision schedule	Copy of schedule and monitoring by administration	By Sept. 1 and ongoing
5. Improve staff monitoring of student behaviors during recess and intramural activities	1. Administration develops and implements a recess and intramural activities supervision schedule	Copy of schedule and monitoring by administration	By Sept. 1 and ongoing
	2. Counselor implements a conflict managers program during recess	Counselor schedule	By Oct. 1

FIGURE 5.7—*continued*

Sample School Action Plan: Monitoring

6. Improve staff monitoring of student behaviors in the hallways	1. Administration develops and implements a hallway supervision schedule	Copy of schedule and monitoring by administration	By Sept. 1 and ongoing
7. Improve staff monitoring of student behaviors before and after school	1. Administration develops and implements a before- and after-school supervision schedule	Copy of schedule and monitoring by administration	By Sept. 1 and ongoing

CHAPTER SIX

Action Plans for Consequences

Classroom Action Plan for Consequences

Sara has a relationships score of 76 percent, a parameters score of 70 percent, and a monitoring score of 80 percent—but her consequences score is 30 percent. Although Sara is an excellent teacher, she believes that giving students consequences undermines her relationships with them. Yet even the best prevention-based approaches to discipline will never eliminate the need for effective consequences.

Here are some steps Sara can take to ensure a more comprehensive approach to classroom management.

Step 1. Identify specific low-scoring areas. After looking more closely at the consequences portion of her self-assessment survey, Sara notes that she scored below 5 on the following items:

- I consistently deliver pretaught consequences when students violate rules.
- Prior to delivering a consequence, I make certain that I am calm and unemotional.
- I know and follow the school procedures for making office referrals.
- I know and follow the school procedures for delivering consequences.

As Sara reflects on these areas, she realizes that the reason she gave herself low scores is that she hates to give consequences. She believes students will always behave well as long as they have a positive relationship with her. However, over the past year she has observed that several students engage more frequently in negative behaviors. This misbehavior has resulted in loss of productive time-on-task for the rest of the class. In addition, some students have begun to emulate the negative behaviors of these students.

Step 2. Write specific, measurable objectives for each of the identified goal areas. Sara wasn't sure where to begin in writing her objectives, so she did what she has always done to boost her work-related knowledge: she talked with teachers who had strong classroom management skills, took some classroom management classes, and read the research. Through this process, she began to change her personal philosophy: where it used to be totally relationship-oriented, it was now more balanced and focused on all of the components of discipline.

When reflecting on the first of the low-scoring areas—remaining calm and unemotional prior to giving a consequence to a student—Sara admitted to herself that, on the rare occasion when she did give a consequence, she was so disappointed with the student that she took it personally. Rather than simply state the rule violation and the consequence, she would launch into a diatribe that took time away from classroom instruction. She also realized that the offending student would tune her out after the first five minutes or so of her lecture. Based on her readings and classes concerning classroom management, Sara came to realize that this approach was ineffective and counterproductive.

Step 3. Develop an action plan including data that indicates progress. After reading the research, conferring with other professionals, and taking some professional development classes, Sara drafted the action plan in Figure 6.1.

Sara developed the rules for her classroom based on classes she attended and conferences with other teachers, then reviewed them with her students. These rules were as follows:

- Always follow teacher directives.
- Follow all rules of conduct.
- Speak quietly.
- Keep your hands to yourselves.

FIGURE 6.1
Sample Teacher Action Plan: Consequences

Goal	Action Steps	Evaluation Data	When
1. Improve consequence component of classroom management	1. When giving consequences to students, do so calmly and unemotionally	Log and discipline records	Daily
	2. Determine and teach the classroom rules	List of rules and lesson plans	By Sept. 15
	3. Follow through with students when there are rule violations using the pre-taught consequences	Log and discipline records	Daily
	4. Review the building criteria for office referrals with students	Lesson plans	By Sept. 15
	5. Follow the building criteria for making office referrals	Log and discipline records	Ongoing
	6. Review the building criteria for using lunch detention, after-school detention, and Friday school with students	Lesson plans	By Sept. 15
	7. Follow the buildingwide rules for using consequences	Log and discipline records	Ongoing

Sara taught her rules through lessons, just as she did with other subject matter, because she knew that students learn better this way. For example, when teaching the rule "always follow teacher directives," she practiced giving directions to see how quickly the students could comply: "Put your pencils down and look at me," "Put your materials away," "Row one, quietly line up by the door." She monitored and provided students with feedback on their performance.

Sara also reviewed specific rules with students whenever their behavior indicated that they were forgetting the rules; clarified terms such as "teacher directives," "rules of conduct," and "quietly"; taught the students each of the academic and special situation rules of conduct; and reviewed the building criteria for office referrals, lunch detention, after-school detention, and Friday school. Because of her strong belief in positive relationships, implementing the discipline program was difficult for Sara. However, she came to believe that without calmly and consistently following through with consequences when necessary, she was contributing to a decline in the positive classroom climate. Sara now believes that it is vital to use consequences when necessary. Maintaining her classroom discipline records and daily log helps her monitor her progress in this area.

Step 4. Analyze the data and make adjustments to the plan. Sara knows how important it is to monitor her progress, so she reviews her log and discipline records weekly. In doing so, she notices that she gets emotional and lectures her students less often now. She attributes this change to a decision to first use nonverbal interventions (e.g., ignoring, monitoring) when students misbehave. When nonverbal interventions don't work, she moves on to verbal interventions (e.g., inferential statements, calling the student's name, asking questions). If the students continue to misbehave, she moves on to demands. Finally, if demands don't work, she calmly and privately gives a consequence appropriate to the offense.

Sara closely monitored her use of office referrals, even though she rarely used them. She found that when she did, the referrals were based on the school criteria. For example, when a student assaulted another student in her classroom, Sara separated the students, conducted some initial fact finding, and sent the offending student to the office, where in the past she would have dealt with the situation entirely on her own. Figure 6.2 shows an excerpt of the discipline log that Sara used to record the student misbehaviors and their consequences.

FIGURE 6.2
Sample Classroom Discipline Log

Date	Time	Student	Infraction	Consequence
10-3-05	10:00 a.m.	John Jones	Tardiness	Lunch detention
10-28-05	2:00 p.m.	Sam Lewis	Insubordination	After-school detention
1-10-06	11:00 a.m.	John Jones	Assault	Office referral

The final step for Sara will be to retake the self-assessment survey at the end of the year and compare her new results with the old ones. Chances are strong that her scores will significantly improve. If they continue to be low, once again she will need to set goals for the following year.

School Action Plan for Consequences

Now consider a school with high scores in the areas of relationships, parameters, and monitoring, but a very low score of 20 percent in the area of consequences. The school discipline committee committed to working all year to determine where the specific needs were, develop and implement a plan, and make ongoing assessments and adjustments as needed. The graphic in Figure 6.3 shows how the continuous improvement cycle of a school is never finished—there will always be areas needing improvement.

FIGURE 6.3
The Schoolwide Discipline Continuous Improvement Cycle

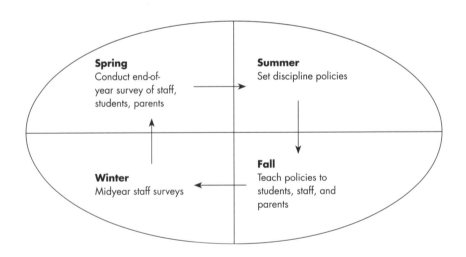

Spring
Conduct end-of-year survey of staff, students, parents

Summer
Set discipline policies

Winter
Midyear staff surveys

Fall
Teach policies to students, staff, and parents

Monthly: Meetings regarding discipline issues

Here are some steps that this school can use to address consequences issues.

Step 1. Identify specific low-scoring areas. The school discipline committee looked at the staff surveys regarding consequences and found that the following items received scores lower than 5:

- Staff members deliver consequences to all students, not just their own.
- Consequences are impossible for students to skip.
- Consequences are timely.
- Consequences are varied enough to suit rule violations of differing severity.
- Consequences are easy to implement.
- When students are referred to the office, communication between staff members and administration is timely and meaningful.
- When students are referred to the office, the consequences they receive are timely and meaningful.
- Staff members have reviewed the guidelines for what constitutes an appropriate office referral.
- Staff members do not overuse office referrals.

In the parent surveys, the following items received scores below 5:

- Staff members appear to do a good job of enforcing school rules.
- Staff members contact parents in a timely manner when discipline issues develop.
- Administrators deliver quick and meaningful consequences during office referrals.

About a third of the students at the school were surveyed as well, and were most likely to consider the following statements false on their surveys:

- Students know what kinds of behaviors will result in office referrals.
- Staff members are visible throughout the school.
- Students behave well in the hallways.
- Students are rarely tardy.
- Very few students act like bullies at school.
- Our school provides appropriate consequences for student misbehaviors.

- All the teachers at our school enforce the school rules.
- Staff members have taught the school rules to students.
- Students at our school are unable to skip the consequences they receive when they break rules.
- When students break rules, they know that they will receive a timely consequence.

The discipline committee decided to conduct observations in September to gather more information on these areas of concern. Three members of the discipline committee were released from their classroom duties for an entire day for this purpose. Figure 6.4 shows an example of the observation form they used.

In addition to conducting observations, two members of the discipline committee were released from their classroom duties to interview random staff members regarding the concerns identified in the surveys (see Figure 6.5).

After reviewing the surveys and observation and interview forms, representatives of the discipline committee attended discipline workshops, visited schools with reputations for outstanding discipline programs, and read several books that were recommended in the workshops. Members made a concerted effort to include other staff members in these activities and keep them updated on their progress. After completing their research, they were ready to draft a plan to share with the entire staff.

Step 2. Write specific, measurable objectives for each of the low-scoring areas identified in step 1.

Step 3. Develop an action plan. If a school has as many problem areas as the one in this chapter does, staff should not take on too many changes at one time. It would probably be advisable for our sample school to implement processing and lunch detention at the beginning of the year, and wait until the middle of the year to implement after-school detention and Friday school.

Figure 6.6 shows an action plan that the discipline committee at our sample school might develop.

FIGURE 6.4

Sample Staff Observation Form for
School Action Plan: Consequences

Date: 2-10-07 to 2-15-07

Look-Fors	Observer Comments
Tardies	Over 30 students in the halls throughout the building before school after the bell rang; students sent to the office, but no detentions assigned by staff; about 20 students tardy to class throughout the day
Hallways	Five students running in the hallway with no consequences; 10 students using profanity with no consequences; 5 students bullying with no consequences
Lunch detention	Total of 30 students in 3 lunch detentions; 10 students talking with no consequences; 5 students acting insubordinately with no consequences; infractions included no work turned in, insubordination, tardiness, noncompliance, and fighting; 5 students in lunch detention for 2 weeks; 3 students did not show up for detention
After-school detention	Total of 15 students in after-school detention; 5 students talking with no consequence; infractions included insubordination, fighting, and noncompliance; 5 students had been in after-school detention for a week; 5 students did not show up for detention
Friday school	Total of 5 students present and 3 no-shows; 3 of 5 students talking rather than working on assignments
Office referrals	20 students observed waiting for consequences from administration throughout the day, with up to 5 waiting at one time; longest wait was 40 minutes; no written referrals from staff (students expected to report offenses themselves)
Student respect	10 students making disrespectful comments to staff members in the hall; 5 students making disrespectful comments to staff members in class; no consequences given for disrespectful comments; numerous students making disrespectful comments to other students
Bullying	See comments for hallways
Lunchtime	Total of 15 students throwing food over 3 lunch periods; 10 students running during lunch; 5 students not complying with staff directives; no consequences given

FIGURE 6.5
Sample Follow-Up Staff Interview Form: Consequences

Date: 2-12-07

Certificated or Classified Staff Member? _____

Do you have any comments or concerns about consequences in the following areas?

○ Buildingwide consequences:

We only have lunch or after-school detention if staff individually assign and supervise it; the only buildingwide consequence is office referral.

○ Office referrals:

Criteria are not clear; referrals are made for varying and inconsistent reasons.

○ Communication during office referrals:

There is no clear system in place for communication; some teachers call the office, some write notes, no standard form is used; staff often don't know what consequences students receive.

○ Consequences during office referrals:

Consequences are inconsistent from student to student; there is no clear hierarchy of consequences; consequences are often implemented two or three days after the referral.

○ Parent communication:

There is no set policy regarding administrator-parent communication; teachers are kept in the dark.

○ Student respect:

About 10 percent of students are extremely disrespectful to staff members; there are no consequences for disrespectful behaviors other than office referrals, and follow-up is inconsistent.

FIGURE 6.5—*continued*

Sample Follow-Up Staff Interview Form: Consequences

Date: 2-12-07

Certificated or Classified Staff Member? _____

Do you have any comments or concerns about consequences in the following areas?

○ Bullying:

About 30 percent of students report to staff that they are bullied on a regular basis by a small number of students; there are no policies or consequences for bullying behaviors.

○ Tardies:

Students are often tardy to class in the morning, and many are late between classes; there is no consequence for tardies other than office referrals; there are no set policies regarding tardies.

○ Hallway behaviors:

Tardies are the biggest concern, but there is also running, yelling, and bullying; there are no consequences other than office referrals.

○ Lunchtime behaviors:

Of the three lunch periods, the first has the best student behavior; the other two periods are loud, with students throwing food and running; there are no consequences other than office referrals.

○ Student recognition programs:

There are no buildingwide student recognition programs, although some teachers have their own recognition programs in their classrooms.

○ Staff support of building rules:

Staff members do not enforce the school rules consistently; some only enforce rules they agree with, others never discipline students they like.

FIGURE 6.6

Sample School Action Plan: Consequences

Goal	Action Steps	Evaluation Data	When
1. Develop conse-quences that are easy to implement, impossible to skip, timely, varied enough to meet rule violations of differing severity	1. Staff develops and implements build-ingwide processing policies	Feedback from staff	By Sept. 15
	2. Staff develops and implements lunch detention	Detention forms	By Sept. 15
	3. Staff develops and implements after-school detention	Detention forms	By Feb. 1
	4. Staff develops and implements Friday school	Detention forms	By Feb. 15
2. Improve the effective-ness of office referrals	1. Administration clarifies office referral criteria	Criteria list	By Sept. 15
	2. Administration communicates office referral criteria to all staff, students, and parents	Staff bul-letin, staff meeting min-utes, parent letter	By Sept. 15
	3. Staff follows criteria for office referrals	Office discipline records	Ongoing
3. Improve communica-tions with staff and parents regard-ing office referrals	1. Administration clarifies expectations for communicating discipline infractions from staff to office and from office to staff and parents	Written expecta-tions, staff and parent newsletters, staff meeting minutes	By Sept. 15
	2. Administration explains the new office referral communication system to staff, students, and parents	Staff meet-ing agenda and minutes	By Oct. 1
	3. Staff implements the new office refer-ral communication system	Office discipline records	By Oct. 2

FIGURE 6.6—*continued*

Sample School Action Plan: Consequences

Goal	Action Steps	Evaluation Data	When
4. Develop and implement a system that rewards as many students as possible for positive behaviors	1. Discipline committee develops a buildingwide reward system for positive student behaviors	Positive reward system	By Oct. 10
	2. Discipline committee communicates positive reward system to coworkers, students, and parents	Staff, parent, student newsletters and staff meeting minutes	By Oct. 30
	3. Staff implements positive reward system		By Nov. 1
5. Teach the rules and consequences to all staff, students, and parents	1. Discipline committee determines buildingwide rules and consequences	List of rules and consequences	By Sept. 1
	2. Discipline committee teaches all staff buildingwide rules and consequences	Staff meeting minutes	By Sept. 1
	3. Discipline committee conducts "rule assemblies" for all students	Staff newsletter	By Sept. 10
	4. Teachers conduct classroom lessons regarding buildingwide rules	Lesson plans	By Sept. 10
6. Improve staff visibility	1. Administrators develop staff supervision schedule for before school, lunchtime, and after school	Staff supervision schedule	By Sept. 1
	2. Administrators monitor staff supervision	Administrator's schedule	Weekly
	3. Administrators monitor their own visibility throughout the week	Administrator's schedule	Weekly
7. Decrease number of student tardies	1. Discipline committee defines tardiness and develops consequences for it	Discipline plan	By Sept. 1
	2. Discipline committee sets goal for fewer tardies and determines individual and group rewards for meeting the goal	Discipline plan	By Sept. 1

(continued)

FIGURE 6.6—*continued*

Sample School Action Plan: Consequences

Goal	Action Steps	Evaluation Data	When
	3. Administrators and discipline committee communicate definition of tardiness, consequences for tardiness, and rewards for fewer tardies to all staff, students, and parents	Student and parent handbook, parent newsletters, assembly schedule, staff meeting minutes	By Sept. 15
	4. Staff enforces consequences and rewards for tardiness	Administrator observations, discipline records	Weekly
8. Increase student-to-student and student-to-staff respect	1. Discipline committee develops respect rubric	Respect rubric	By Sept. 1
	2. Discipline committee teaches respect rubric to all staff, students, and parents	Lesson plans, staff meeting minutes, parent newsletter	By Sept. 30
	3. Discipline committee adds disrespectful behaviors to discipline plan	Discipline plan	By Sept. 1
	4. Discipline committee adds respectful behaviors to reward system	Reward system	By Sept. 1
	5. Staff implements consequences and rewards related to respect	Discipline records, administration observations	Weekly
9. Decrease bullying behaviors	1. Students take bullying survey	Bullying survey	By Sept. 30
	2. Discipline committee analyzes results of surveys and develops plan	Anti-bullying plan	By Oct. 30
	3. Students retake bullying survey	Bullying survey	By June 10

FIGURE 6.6—*continued*

Sample School Action Plan: Consequences

Goal	Action Steps	Evaluation Data	When
	4. Discipline committee analyzes results of survey and revises plan for following year	New anti-bullying plan	By Sept. 1 next year
10. Ensure that all staff consistently enforce all rules with all the students	1. Staff members self-monitor rule enforcement	Self-reflections	Daily
	2. Students, staff, and parents take discipline surveys	Staff, student, and parent discipline surveys	Midyear and end of year
	3. Administrators monitor staff enforcement of discipline policies	Administration log	Daily
	4. Administrators follow up with staff members who inconsistently enforce discipline policies	Conferences, discipline letters, plans for improvement, evaluations	As needed
11. Improve student behaviors during lunchtime	1. Discipline committee develops expectations and consequences for student behaviors during lunchtime	List of lunch expectations and consequences	By Sept. 1
	2. Staff teaches students expectations and consequences for lunchtime behaviors	Lesson plans	By end of first day of school
	3. Administrators review lunchtime expectations and consequences with all students	School schedule	On first day of school
	4. Staff monitors students' behaviors during lunchtime	Discipline data	Daily
	5. Staff implements consequences as necessary for inappropriate lunch behaviors	Lunchtime detention data	Daily

Because our sample school is a middle school, the action plan does not address discipline issues related to recess. Figure 6.7 shows what action steps an elementary school might take in this regard.

Figure 6.8 shows the hierarchy of consequences that we recommend for schools, beginning with processing at the bottom and ending with office referrals at the top.

Processing

"Processing" refers to a 10- to 15-minute time out in another classroom. During this time, students reflect on and write about what they did to receive the processing consequence, what rules they broke, and how they need to behave when they return to class. Processing has many advantages: it is immediate, allows teachers to deal proactively with the smallest classroom disruptions, and can head off more serious misbehavior. At the same time, it ought to be backed with more serious consequences, such as lunch or recess detention. We strongly encourage that processing be implemented throughout the school, with each teacher having a "buddy teacher" to whom he or she can send students.

As with all consequences, it is critical to teach students what behaviors will result in processing, and what the consequence entails. All classrooms should be set up with a desk and forms for processing in an easily accessed area away from other students. Students should be taught that they are expected to be nondisruptive and complete their processing forms (see Figure 6.9). If students misbehave during processing, they must be given a more serious consequence, such as lunch or after-school detention. Students are also responsible for making up any work missed during processing. Ideally, only one student should be in processing at any given time; if there are more, they should not interact. Examples of criteria for receiving processing include minor talk-outs, off-task behaviors, and minor noncompliance.

Lunch or Recess Detention

Lunch and recess detentions are usually held in rooms set aside for that purpose. Schools may choose to implement either form of detention as a consequence, though some schools implement both. Examples of criteria for lunch or recess detention are disruptions during processing,

FIGURE 6.7
Sample School Action Plan: Consequences (Recess)

Goal	Action Steps	Evaluation Data	When
1. Improve student behaviors during recess	1. Administration develops and communicates recess supervision schedule	Supervision schedule	By Sept. 1
	2. Discipline committee identifies expectations and consequences for student behaviors during recess	Recess plan	By Sept. 1
	3. Discipline committee develops and staff implements recess detention system	Detention plan	By Sept. 1
	4. Staff teaches recess expectations and consequences to students	Lesson plans	By end of first week
	5. Administrators review recess expectations and consequences with students	School schedule	By end of first week
	6. Counselor develops and implements recess student conflict management plan	Counselor plans and recess schedule	By Oct. 1
	7. Assigned staff monitors students' behaviors during recess and implements consequences	Discipline records	Ongoing
	8. Physical education teacher makes and implements a plan for student activities during recess	Physical education plan	By Sept. 15
	9. Physical education teacher teaches students rules for student activities during recess	Lesson plans	By Sept. 15

lunchroom disturbances, classroom disturbances, tardies, and gum chewing in class. To prevent students from skipping detention, teachers should escort them to the detention room. If the detention room is centrally located, it should be easy for the teacher to drop the students off while walking the rest of the students to lunch or recess.

As with processing, there should be clear expectations for student behavior during detention. If students are disruptive during detention, or if they don't change their ways, they should automatically be assigned to after-school detention. When the administrators notice a

FIGURE 6.8
Hierarchy of Consequences

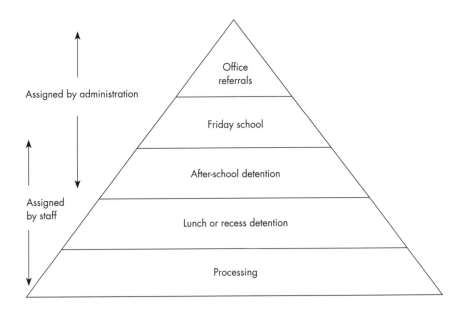

pattern or a repeat offender, they should hold a conference with the student's teacher to determine whether a more effective consequence can be put in place.

The staff member who supervises detention must be a strong disciplinarian. He or she must be very clear in stating expectations, monitoring students' behaviors, and implementing additional consequences as needed. We have seen examples of supervisors who let students watch television, talk, and walk around. These detention rooms are ineffective and basically a waste of resources. The detention room will only be as effective as the supervisor in charge.

After-School Detention

After-school detention is typically between 45 minutes and one hour in length. Teachers usually assign after-school detention for academic issues, minor noncompliance, misbehavior with substitute teachers,

FIGURE 6.9
Sample Processing Form

Name: _____ Date: _____

Time sent back to class: _____

How many times have you been processed this week? _____

What time is it now? _____

What did you do?

_____

_____

Why did you make this decision?

_____ I wanted attention from others.

_____ I wanted to be in control of the situation.

_____ I wanted to challenge the teacher's authority.

_____ I wanted to avoid doing my schoolwork.

_____ I don't know what I'm supposed to be doing.

_____ I wanted revenge.

_____ I was not prepared for class.

Other:

_____

_____

How did your behavior affect you?

_____

_____

How did your behavior affect the teacher and the other students?

_____

_____

Why is this kind of behavior unacceptable?

_____

_____

Name two things you are going to do to improve your behavior:

_____

_____

If you go back to the classroom and your behavior continues to be disruptive, what consequences should you receive?

_____

_____

disruptions during lunch detention, chronic tardiness, and cumulative violations. Administrators usually assign after-school detention for serious rule violations, cumulative violations, and for most office referrals.

As with lunch and recess detention, we recommend that teachers drop students off for after-school detention so that they cannot skip the consequence. In some cases, students may be assigned work during after-school detention. If a student misbehaves during detention, a more serious consequence such as Friday school or suspension should be considered.

Friday School

We believe that teachers should be empowered to assign lunch, recess, and after-school detention after they have determined and communicated clear criteria. However, we believe Friday school should only be assigned by administrators.

Friday school typically lasts two to three hours after school on Fridays. Examples of criteria for Friday school include skipping detention, recurring discipline offenses, six or more tardies, sexual harassment, and severe noncompliance. If students misbehave during Friday school, they should be told that they could face suspension.

Administrators must monitor which students are receiving what consequences for what behaviors, and how often. Not all consequences are effective for all students. Some teachers "bury" students in detention "until further notice." When this happens, it's usually because teachers are frustrated and don't know what else to do. In such cases, administrators may wish to hold strategy meetings with the teachers.

Office Referrals

At the top of the consequence hierarchy are office referrals, which should be reserved for the most serious rule violations. Possible reasons for office referrals include physical threats, violent or gang-related behavior, blatant noncompliance, sexual harassment, and serious disruptions of the educational process. Administrators should discuss the criteria for office referrals with students and staff, clarifying what each term means. (In schools with a prevalence of gang issues, staff may benefit from training from the local police.)

There should be an excellent communication system in place for office referrals, with everyone who needs to know about the referral being informed in a timely manner. This process begins with the referring teacher personally contacting the administrator about the student's disruptive behavior. The administrator then determines the consequence for the misbehavior and contacts the parent. Following this, the administrator contacts the referring teacher and summarizes the intervention. If the student has more than one teacher, all of the student's teachers receive a summary of the referral and results. There is no such thing as over-communication; the best communication is verbal and immediate, either face-to-face or over the phone. If this is not possible, a consistent referral form should be used.

The minimal consequence for appropriate office referrals is two nights of after-school detention, and the consequence should be swiftly applied, so that the office does not become a "holding tank" for students. When there are a number of students in the office for referrals, every attempt should be made to keep them separated and invisible to visitors to the office. Teachers usually don't mind if a student returns to the classroom after an office referral as long as a meaningful consequence has been communicated.

See Figure 6.10 for a list of appropriate consequences for different rule violations.

Reward Systems

We recommend that for every consequence, there be one reward system. Because there are five major consequences—processing, lunch or recess detention, after-school detention, Friday school, and office referrals—there should therefore be five reward systems. Staff members should determine what specific behaviors they want to positively reinforce. For example, if "respect" is a school goal, staff should reward students for displaying respectful behaviors. One idea is for staff to hand out "respect tickets" when students are seen acting respectfully. The students put their names on the tickets and then put them in a designated location, such as a box in the library. Tickets are then drawn from the box at random times, and students whose tickets are selected get to attend special activities (e.g., pizza with the principal or a movie

FIGURE 6.10
Appropriate Consequences for Selected Rule Violations

Rule Violation	Consequence
Minor disruptions	*Processing*
Minor talkouts	*Processing*
Gum chewing	*Lunch or recess detention*
Tardiness	*Lunch or recess detention*
Classroom disturbances	*After-school detention*
Minor noncompliance	*After-school detention*
Cumulative violations	*After-school detention or Friday school*
Incomplete work	*After-school detention or Friday school*
Physical threats	*Office referral and suspension*
Violent behavior	*Office referral and suspension*
Serious classroom disruptions	*Office referral and suspension*
Blatant noncompliance	*Office referral and suspension*
Gang-related behavior	*Office referral and suspension*
Vandalism	*Office referral and suspension*
Sexual harassment	*Office referral and suspension*

showing) or receive citizenship certificates at assemblies. The reward system should recognize as many students as possible.

Teaching the Rules

It is common in schools for administrators to assume that everyone knows what the rules and attendant consequences are, or that handing out a discipline handbook is sufficient. It is important to distribute a list of rules and consequences to staff, students, and parents, but that is not enough; rules should be taught and retaught, not just to students but also to staff members. All too often, new staff members have no idea what the rules are, or veteran staff forget rules that don't seem important to them. Consistency is key, and a school cannot be consistent if staff and students don't know what the common expectations are. Simply developing and distributing a supervision schedule is also not enough; administrators must monitor staff members to ensure that they are following the schedule and must deal with individuals who miss their assignments.

Step 4. Analyze the data and make adjustments to the plan. The issue here is the same as with the other components: the discipline committee, administration, and staff must monitor and assess implementation of the plan. Although the discipline committee is charged with taking the lead in this effort, the entire staff needs to be brought into the loop as appropriate and contribute to analyzing the results and making adjustments when necessary.

CHAPTER SEVEN

Improvement Plans for Teachers Struggling with Discipline Issues

The action plans for individual teachers given in the previous chapters are based on the assumption that the teachers and not the administration initiate the plans, based on self-reflection and self-evaluation. This is the ideal; in reality, however, many teachers who need to improve their classroom management have neither the capability nor the motivation to analyze their weaknesses honestly and make a plan for improvement on their own.

Administrators must be able to tell the difference between fundamentally unsatisfactory teachers and those who are merely inexperienced and thus have the potential to improve. According to Danielson (1996), there are four different levels of performance: unsatisfactory, basic, proficient, and distinguished. In our experience, the difference between unsatisfactory teachers and those who are simply inexperienced comes down to teacher attitude. Teachers with potential for improvement will try whatever their supervisors suggest and will work hard to gain skills, whereas those who are fundamentally unsatisfactory will spend their time making excuses and resisting change instead.

Platt, Tripp, Ogden, and Fraser (2000) recommend that administrators working with unsatisfactory teachers obtain data from multiple sources, ask hard questions, and pay close attention to the answers. The norm of excellence must be nonnegotiable. Extensive training and ongoing discussions with staff about what good classroom management looks like is critical, so that everyone is clear on the norms.

When helping a teacher create a plan for improvement, administrators need to work closely with the district office, the teachers union, and the school district's attorney. If the possibility that the teacher may be fired exists, the district office needs to be involved so that the administrator has support and guidance. Of course, the goal should always be to help the teacher improve, but sometimes it is clear that a teacher either cannot or will not change his or her behaviors. It is ultimately the teacher's responsibility to embrace the plan for improvement, make it his or her own, and make the necessary changes.

If a teacher is to be fired, it is critical to involve the union, as there are timelines and processes that need to be followed lest a firing case be thrown out due to procedural errors. Contracts vary as to performance criteria and procedures, so administrators should be aware of the language of the contract for their districts. Involving the union indicates that the administration has nothing to hide.

Following are examples of unsatisfactory teachers struggling in the four component areas of discipline. (Note: Sample contract language is adapted from the teacher contract in Bethel School District, Spanaway, Washington.)

Plan for Improvement: Relationships

According to her survey on relationships, Leslie has difficulty in the following areas:

- Treating all colleagues with dignity and respect
- Actively and consistently supporting school policies
- Working collaboratively with colleagues to resolve student discipline issues
- Informing parents in a timely manner when students have discipline issues
- Sharing classroom rules with parents at the beginning of the school year, then following up as needed
- Getting back to parents as quickly as possible
- Treating all students with dignity and respect
- Always letting students keep their dignity when delivering consequences

The administration has gathered the following specific data on Leslie through observations and at yearly evaluations:

- At staff meetings on Sept. 13, Oct. 30, and March 14, she made the following derogatory comments to coworkers: "That's a stupid thing to say," "If you ever supervised your students you would know that," and "Your class is out of control 90 percent of the time."
- She missed her assigned duties 10 times during the year.
- She failed to return phone calls to at least 13 parents throughout the year.
- She made four students put their noses against the wall as a disciplinary consequence.
- She was observed yelling at students in the halls, at recess, in the library, and in the classroom on at least seven occasions during the year.
- At least 10 students during the year have reported to the health room that they are afraid of her due to her yelling and calling them names.
- Five parents have asked to move their students from her classroom due to yelling and name calling.
- She missed at least five meetings with coworkers during the year.

In reviewing the evaluation section of the teacher's contract, administrators identified the following as areas of unsatisfactory performance and listed them as goal areas for the next year's plan for improvement:

Criterion 2: Classroom Management
A. *Dealing consistently and fairly with students*
B. *Providing a positive classroom learning environment*

Criterion 3: Professional Preparation and Scholarship
A. *Communicating proactively with parents and staff*
B. *Working collaboratively with others for the welfare of students and the school*

Criterion 5: The Handling of Student Discipline and Attendant Problems
A. *Resolving discipline problems in accordance with law, school board policy, and school policies and procedures*
C. *Responding appropriately to disciplinary problems when they occur*

With clear criteria and specific data from past observations and evaluations, the administrator can make a specific plan for improvement for Leslie. Writing the improvement plan should be fairly easy if the final evaluation is well written, addresses evaluative criteria, clearly describes the problem areas and the expected behaviors, and cites specific data that relate to the criteria. When creating an improvement plan, Platt and colleagues (2000) recommend

- Establishing a team (e.g., a group including a support teacher, a consultant, and a union representative).
- Developing goals for improvement.
- Selecting activities and strategies that are specific and assessable and have a timetable.
- Assigning responsibility for data-collection sources.
- Establishing evidence of progress.

Figure 7.1 shows an example of an improvement plan that would address Leslie's issues with relationships.

Plan for Improvement: Parameters

Keri has problems in the area of setting parameters of acceptable student behavior. Issues of concern from Keri's parameters survey included the following:

- Teaching academic rules of conduct until all students consistently comply with them
- Teaching classroom rules of conduct until all students consistently comply with them
- Teaching special situation rules of conduct until all students consistently comply with them
- Teaching the school rules until all students consistently comply with them
- Testing students to be certain they understand the classroom discipline plan and rules of conduct
- Reteaching the classroom discipline plan and rules of conduct whenever students seem to have forgotten them
- Reviewing the rationale behind each rule

FIGURE 7.1

Improvement Plan: Relationships

Identified Problem	Corrective Action	Evaluation Data	Support Structures
Criterion 2 **Classroom Management** A. Dealing consistently and fairly with students B. Providing a positive classroom learning environment *In the past year, Leslie has used inappropriate consequences with students and has not treated students with dignity and respect. The atmosphere in the classroom is often negative and oppressive. Parents and students have reported incidents of Leslie calling students inappropriate names and yelling at them.*	Consistently and fairly respond to inappropriate behaviors by students at all times. Follow the school policies regarding positive rewards and consequences at all times. Take an administrator-approved workshop on positive discipline strategies approved by December. Read two administrator-approved books on classroom management. Do not receive negative reports from parents, staff, or students regarding inappropriate behaviors.	Classroom observation reports Reports from students, parents, and other staff members Classroom and building discipline records Confirmation of workshop attendance Conversations with supervisor regarding classroom management books Complaints from staff, students, and parents	Observation summaries Conferences with supervisor Classroom management workshop Copy of school discipline plan At least two classroom management books At least two days of release time to observe teachers modeling appropriate classroom management

FIGURE 7.1—*continued*

Improvement Plan: Relationships

Identified Problem	Corrective Action	Evaluation Data	Support Structures
Criterion 3 **Professional Preparation and Scholarship** A. Communicating proactively with parents and staff B. Working collaboratively with others for the welfare of students and the school *Leslie has been observed making negative comments to and about coworkers. She has failed to return many parent phone calls and to proactively call parents regarding student progress and behavior.* *She has also failed to meet many building supervision responsibilities, and misses problem-solving meetings with coworkers.*	Cease making negative comments about and toward students and coworkers. Return all parent phone calls promptly. Proactively call parents regarding performance and behavior issues. Consistently meet building supervision responsibilities as scheduled. Consistently attend all meetings with coworkers to discuss student issues.	Reports from coworkers, parents, and students Log kept by supervisor Phone log School supervision schedules Monitoring by supervisor Meeting minutes Letters of instruction	Modeling and role playing by supervisor Feedback from supervisor Sample phone log School supervision schedule
Criterion 5 **The Handling of Student Discipline and Attendant Problems** A. Resolving discipline problems in accordance with law, school board policy, and school policies and procedures C. Responding appropriately to disciplinary problems when they occur *Leslie failed to follow the school discipline plan for rewards and consequences, and has often used inappropriate self-determined consequences with students.*	Consistently follow district and school discipline policies and procedures. Cease use of self-determined negative consequences for student behaviors. Consistently use positive reward systems for appropriate student behaviors.	Observation summaries Reports from staff, parents, and students Approved positive reward system and log of use	At least two days of release time to observe teachers modeling appropriate classroom management At least two classroom management books Classroom management workshop

The administration gathered the following data to share with Keri during the latter's end-of-the-year evaluation:

- Keri did not follow through with the school plan of teaching academic, classroom, or special situation rules of conduct.
- She did not follow through with the school plan for teaching the school's rules and policies.
- The teacher did not test all students on the school discipline program.

In reviewing the evaluation section of the teacher's contract, the administration identified the following goal areas for Keri's improvement plan:

Criterion 2: Classroom Management
C. Teaching appropriate behavior, establishing and teaching reasonable rules

Criterion 3: Professional Preparation and Scholarship
B. Working collaboratively with others for the welfare of students and the school
C. Supporting district and school learning goals

Criterion 5: The Handling of Student Discipline and Attendant Problems
B. Establishing clear parameters for student in-classroom conduct and making known these expectations

Figure 7.2 shows an example of an improvement plan that would address Keri's issues with setting parameters.

Plan for Improvement: Monitoring

Pete has problems in the area of monitoring student behavior. Issues of concern from Pete's monitoring survey included the following:

- Consistently and effectively using monitoring skills in the classroom with all students
- Being visible in the halls during transition periods
- Monitoring student behaviors in assemblies

FIGURE 7.2
Improvement Plan: Parameters

Identified Problem	Corrective Action	Evaluation Data	Support Structures
Criterion 2 **Classroom Management** C. Teaching appropriate behavior, establishing and teaching reasonable rules *Keri did not create or teach a classroom discipline plan to her students. As a result, students were unclear about behavioral expectations.*	Create and teach classroom discipline plan to students by Sept. 15. Reteach classroom discipline plan as necessary throughout the year.	Written classroom discipline plan Observation summaries Lesson plans	Observation summaries Conferences with supervisor Classroom management workshop selected by the district At least two books on classroom management At least two days of release time to observe teachers determined by supervisor
Criterion 3 **Professional Preparation and Scholarship** B. Working collaboratively with others for the welfare of students and the school C. Supporting district and school learning goals *Keri did not teach students the schoolwide discipline plan or test them on it.*	Teach students the schoolwide discipline plan by Sept. 15. Test students on the schoolwide discipline plan by Sept. 20. Reteach the discipline plan to students as necessary.	Lesson plans Classroom observations Test results	Schoolwide discipline plan Sample schoolwide discipline plan test Administrative assistance and guidance as needed
Criterion 5 **The Handling of Student Discipline and Attendant Problems** B. Establishing clear parameters for student in-classroom conduct and making known these expectations *Keri did not establish clear parameters for student conduct, which caused students to be unclear regarding behavioral expectations.*	See Criterion 2 above.	See Criterion 2 above.	See Criterion 2 above.

The administration gathered the following data to share with Pete during his end-of-the-year evaluation:

- During a classroom observation, he was seen sitting at his desk while students did independent seatwork and at least 30 percent of students were off task, visiting, talking, and being disruptive.
- He was observed in the halls during passing periods only in the first week of school.
- On seven occasions, he was observed standing on the floor during assemblies rather than sitting with students, which is building policy.

In reviewing the evaluation section of Pete's contract, the administration identified the following goal areas for next year's improvement plan:

Criterion 2: Classroom Management
C. Monitoring student behaviors

Criterion 3: Professional Preparation and Scholarship
B. Working collaboratively with others for the welfare of students and the school
C. Supporting district and school learning goals

Criterion 5: The Handling of Student Discipline and Attendant Problems
D. Proactively recognizing conditions which may lead to disciplinary problems
E. Developing appropriate strategies for preventing disciplinary problems

Figure 7.3 shows an example of an improvement plan that would address Pete's issues with monitoring.

Plan for Improvement: Consequences

Amy has problems in the area of consequences. Issues of concern from Amy's consequences survey included the following:

- Consistently administering pretaught consequences when students violate rules

FIGURE 7.3
Improvement Plan: Monitoring

Identified Problem	Corrective Action	Evaluation Data	Support Structures
Criterion 2 **Classroom Management** C. Monitoring student behaviors *Pete does not consistently or effectively monitor students in the classroom or throughout the school. As a result, students are often off task in the classroom and misbehave in hallways and in assemblies.*	Consistently and effectively use monitoring skills in the classroom with all students. Remain visible in the halls during transition periods at least three days a week. Sit with students during assemblies and monitor their behaviors.	Formal and informal observations in the classroom and throughout the school Staff and student reports	Classroom management workshop At least one release day to observe an administration-selected teacher Conferences with and observation summaries from administration
Criterion 3 **Professional Preparation and Scholarship** B. Collaborating with others for welfare of students and the school C. Supporting district and school learning goals *Pete does not consistently follow the school policies for monitoring students.*	Follow school policies for monitoring students during transition periods and in assemblies.	Formal and informal observations Staff reports	Copy of school discipline plan Discussion and clarification of discipline plan by administration Schedule of assemblies
Criterion 5 **The Handling of Student Discipline and Attendant Problems** D. Proactively recognizing conditions which may lead to disciplinary problems E. Developing appropriate strategies for preventing disciplinary problems *Pete does not proactively monitor students' behaviors in the classroom or in other areas of the school. As a result, students are often off task or misbehaving.*	See Criterion 2 above. Develop and implement a plan for monitoring student behaviors in the classroom. Develop and implement a plan for monitoring student behaviors in the hallways and during assemblies.	Formal and informal observations in the classroom and throughout the school Classroom plan Hallway plan Assembly plan	Discussions with administration Feedback by administration

- Selecting consequences that suit the violation at hand
- Remaining calm and unemotional when giving consequences to students
- Allowing students to keep their dignity when delivering consequences
- Following the school procedures for making office referrals
- Following the school procedures for delivering consequences

The administration gathered the following data to share with Amy during her end-of-the-year evaluation:

- She was observed yelling at students three times during the year.
- On at least five occasions, she delivered disciplinary consequences that were not in accordance with school policies.
- On at least seven occasions, she was observed ignoring student misbehaviors in the classroom.

In reviewing the evaluation section of Amy's contract, the administration identified the following goal areas for her improvement plan:

Criterion 2: Classroom Management
A. *Dealing consistently and fairly with students*

Criterion 3: Professional Preparation and Scholarship
B. *Working collaboratively with others for the welfare of students and the school*
C. *Supporting district and school goals*

Criterion 5: The Handling of Student Discipline and Attendant Problems
D. *Responding appropriately to disciplinary problems*
E. *Resolving discipline problems in accordance with law, school board policies, and school policies*
F. *Helping students attain self-discipline*

Figure 7.4 shows an example of an improvement plan that would address Amy's issues with consequences.

FIGURE 7.4

Improvement Plan: Consequences

Identified Problem	Corrective Action	Evaluation Data	Support Structures
Criterion 2 **Classroom Management** A. Dealing consistently and fairly with students *Amy sometimes ignores blatant misbehaviors and publicly humiliates students when delivering consequences. She does not follow the schoolwide discipline plan.*	Deliver consequences positively and calmly. Consistently follow the schoolwide discipline plan.	Formal and informal observations Student, staff, and parent reports	Observation of at least one teacher selected by the administration At least one classroom management workshop selected by the district Clarification of the schoolwide discipline plan Observation reports and conferences
Criterion 3 **Professional Preparation and Scholarship** B. Working collaboratively with others for the welfare of students and the school C. Supporting district and school learning goals *Amy does not follow the schoolwide discipline plan.*	Consistently follow the schoolwide discipline plan.	Formal and informal observations Students, staff, and parent reports	Clarification of the schoolwide discipline plan
Criterion 5 **The Handling of Student Discipline and Attendant Problems** D. Responding appropriately to disciplinary problems E. Resolving discipline problems in accordance with the law, school board policies, and school policies F. Helping students attain self-discipline *Amy does not follow the schoolwide discipline plan.*	See Criterion 2 above.	See Criterion 2 above.	See Criterion 2 above.

Though we have presented the above concerns and subsequent plans for improvement as isolated situations, this often is not the case. For example, a teacher with issues related to monitoring skills may also have problems setting parameters of acceptable student behaviors and giving consequences. Creating separate plans for improvement for each component may seem redundant, but in reality it creates a seamless set of expectations for teacher behaviors and increases the likelihood of teacher success.

CHAPTER EIGHT

Action Plans for Challenging Students

E very school has students who are especially difficult to control. Many of these students may have attention deficit disorder (ADD), attention deficit hyperactivity disorder (ADHD), conduct disorder, or oppositional defiant disorder (ODD). According to Rief (1998), 30 to 65 percent of students who have been diagnosed with ADHD also display ODD characteristics. Even more students exhibit these behaviors without having been formally diagnosed. Such students perform best in environments that are predictable, consistent, and structured. In some cases, they need specially designed instruction or 504 plans to help modify their behaviors so they can be successful in school. The goal of these plans is to improve the effectiveness and efficiency of behavioral support for the student.

MacKenzie (1996) notes that ADHD affects 3 to 5 percent of the school-age population and cuts across all socioeconomic, cultural, and ethnic backgrounds (although it affects more boys than girls). Symptoms include increased activity level, impulsivity, and distractibility; difficulty staying focused, following directions, and keeping track of assignments; and a tendency to become easily frustrated and overwhelmed. Symptoms of ODD include frequent aggression, temper tantrums, failure to respect others' property, defiance, refusal to comply with instructions, and repeated displays of resentment (Hall & Hall, 2003). When working with students who have been diagnosed with ADHD or ODD, keep in mind the following:

- Because these students' behaviors are driven by impulse, ignoring the behaviors has little effect.
- Punishments do little to modify ADD, ADHD, or ODD behaviors, and students may be suspicious of praise, equating it with manipulation.
- Students who display ADD, ADHD, or ODD behaviors find long-term goals difficult to attain.
- These students are better behaved when active and task-oriented.
- These students need consistency and structure in their days.

Many students who display the aforementioned behavior patterns will never receive special education services and will remain in the core classroom because they are not formally diagnosed. The Individuals with Disabilities Education Act (IDEA) stipulates that the qualifying category for students with ODD is "severely emotionally disturbed," and the qualifying category for ADHD is "other health impairment." Prior to qualifying for special education services, a long and arduous process must be followed to ascertain that these disabilities are having a profoundly negative effect on the student's education.

The example that follows focuses on an imaginary student who displays many characteristics and symptoms associated with ADD, ADHD, and ODD.

Student Profile

Jason is currently in the 4th grade and is new to his school. He exhibits the following characteristics both at school and at home:

- He is extremely energetic.
- He has difficulty focusing on any one topic for long periods of time.
- He has difficulty completing his homework and often loses it.
- He often blurts out whatever is on his mind at inappropriate times.
- He can become aggressive when frustrated.
- He occasionally displays defiant behavior.

- He is extremely talented artistically: his favorite pastimes are drawing and painting, which he can do with focus and precision for long periods.

Jason's teacher, Jo Ann, has gone to the school's multidisciplinary team (MDT) asking for help dealing with Jason's behaviors. She is a new teacher with strong classroom management skills, but she is quickly becoming frustrated with her inability to deal with Jason effectively. She has found many things to like about him: he is affectionate, personable, charming, artistic, and funny. However, when it comes to following directions and taking part in classroom discussions and routines, he is often disruptive, off task, impulsive, and defiant. Jason's behavior has been disrupting the natural flow of instruction and pacing in the classroom, and Jo Ann is beginning to feel that it is negatively affecting the rest of the class. She has also begun to notice a strain in her relationship with Jason's mother, who accuses her of losing Jason's homework when in fact he doesn't turn it in.

In reviewing records from Jason's previous school, the MDT discovers that, at the end of 3rd grade, Jason was diagnosed as having ADHD with some ODD components. As the family had moved during the summer, no behavior plan had been developed for Jason at his old school. He is currently on prescribed medication for hyperactivity, but medication alone cannot address all of his behavioral and academic issues.

The MDT has had experience with other students with ADHD and realizes the need to develop a plan to address Jason's issues. In order to be successful, the plan should start with small steps and build upon success, as well as encourage a strong, positive working relationship with Jason's parents.

After Jo Ann summarizes her concerns, the team asks her to prioritize them so that they can be approached sequentially. In descending order of importance, she lists the following issues that she has with Jason:

- He calls out without raising his hand or being called on.
- He is sometimes noncompliant and defiant.
- He is sometimes aggressive when frustrated.
- He has difficulty staying on a task for more than 10 minutes.

- He rarely responds to her signals or gives full attention to directions.
- He does not turn in his homework.

When addressing these issues, the goal is to succeed with one action plan before moving on to the next one. In every action plan, the first step is to obtain a baseline of behavior so that Jo Ann can determine whether Jason's behavior improves. The MDT suggests that another staff member be responsible for coming into the classroom and tallying the baseline behavior. Possible staff members to take on this task are administrators, counselors, psychologists, or intervention specialists.

Action plans can be used either as 504 plans or as part of a student's individualized education plan. The plans are divided into three components: the specific goal, the action steps to meet the goal, and various strategies that can be used to help meet the goal.

Following is an example of an action plan that the MDT could develop to help Jason correct rectify his issues with calling out unbidden in class. With minimal adjustments, this plan can be altered to address most behavioral issues.

Sample Action Plan for Raising Hand and Waiting to Be Called On

Goal: Jason should raise his hand and wait to be called on during classroom lectures and discussions.

Action Step 1: Observer obtains baseline behavioral data. A staff member keeps a tally of how often Jason calls out without raising his hand or being called on over a period of at least three days.

Action Step 2: The teacher explains the rules.

1. The teacher meets with Jason and explains the goal and the rationale for the goal (i.e., a rule in her classroom is that all students need to raise their hand and wait to be called on).

2. The teacher explains to Jason that she understands that this is more difficult for him because of the ADHD, but she has every confidence that he will be able to learn and she is willing to help him.

Action Step 3: Implementation.

1. The teacher focuses on one content area at a time. After Jason succeeds in raising his hand and waiting to be called on during the first content area (reading) for an entire week, the teacher focuses on the second content area (math).

2. After Jason succeeds in raising his hand and waiting to be called on during the second content area for an entire week, the teacher focuses on the third content area (science).

3. After Jason succeeds in raising his hand and waiting to be called on during the third content area for an entire week, the goal is for him to raise his hand and wait to be called on throughout the entire day.

Strategies:

- Teacher praise when Jason raises his hand
- Preferential seating (e.g., closer to the teacher's desk)
- Behavior chart for hand-raising
- Incentives for success and consequences for lack of success
- A secret signal from the teacher reminding Jason to raise his hand
- Redirection or reminders when Jason speaks without raising his hand
- Time outs when necessary
- Informing Jason of when he will be called on ahead of time
- A signal from Jason for gaining the teacher's attention appropriately (i.e., placing a card on his desk)

Student Progress Charts

When following an action plan, it is important to maintain a student progress chart (see Figure 8.1). Ideally, the student should help assess how he or she is doing on each step, though of course the ultimate decision is up to the teacher. The teacher should also update the student's parents regularly throughout the process, as building strong relationships between the school and home can positively affect student progress.

FIGURE 8.1
Student Progress Chart

Plan # 1

Baseline: Student raises hand 0 times before being called on.

Reward and reward schedule: Student gets to be line leader after achieving an 80% success rate for every content area in one day.

Consequences and schedule: Teacher reminds student to raise hand after each blurt out.

	Monday	Tuesday	Wednesday	Thursday	Friday
Reading	2 of 5 = 40%	1 of 5 = 20%	4 of 5 = 80%	3 of 5 = 60%	4 of 5 = 80%
Math	1 of 5 = 20%	2 of 5 = 40%	3 of 5 = 60%	5 of 5 = 100%	4 of 5 = 80%
Science	1 of 5 = 20%	2 of 5 = 40%	2 of 5 = 40%	5 of 5 = 100%	4 of 5 = 80%

Rewards and Consequences

Inherent in every action plan is a system of rewards and consequences, which should be determined before the plan is implemented. Following is a list of possible rewards and consequences that can be used with most behavior-related action plans for students.

Possible Rewards

When students engage in positive behaviors, consider the following possible rewards:

- Make private statements of encouragement to the student before and after class
- Give the student positive notes
- Contact parents with praise for the student
- Award class privilege (e.g., being line leader for a week)
- Give the student a choice of seating
- Send the student to the principal or counselor with a positive note
- Give the student a choice of rewards (e.g., extra gym, art, reading, or music time)
- Allow the student to tutor a younger student at the school

- Provide material rewards, such as school supplies, stickers, treasure chest items, books, or coupons
- Allow the student to self-monitor

Possible Consequences

When students engage in negative behaviors, consider the following possible consequences:

- Take away points or stars earned for good behaviors
- Ignore the student for a period of time
- Take away privileges
- Administer a time out
- Reprimand the student verbally, but calmly and quietly

Removal Plan

Every classroom should have a removal plan in place in the event that a student will not leave the classroom when directed to do so. This plan should only be used in extreme cases and should be communicated to everyone involved, including the student's parents. Staff members who are involved in implementing the plan should be trained in restraint strategies. Figure 8.2 shows a sample removal plan.

Working with Parents

When working with parents of students afflicted with ADD, ADHD, or ODD, staff members must remember to act empathetically with them, as the parents are victims of the disabilities as well and thus deserve special help and consideration. (For more information on understanding the difficulties of parenting children with behavioral disabilities, we suggest Nancy Hagener's 2005 book *The Dance of Defiance*.) Here are some guidelines to keep in mind when working with parents:

- The teacher should make positive phone calls to parents on a regular basis. The small amount of time that it takes to do this will often make the parents' day, and will make the teacher's job much easier over the long run.

FIGURE 8.2
Sample Removal Plan

When the student displays behaviors that endanger the safety of others or endangers property, the following steps will be taken:

1. The teacher will contact the office.
2. The office will contact the following designated staff members:

_____

_____

_____

3. The designated staff members will immediately go to the classroom and escort the student to the office.
4. The office will call the student's parents.
5. The teacher will write up a report of the incident.

- When possible, the teacher should ask parents to help review and develop the action plans. Although sometimes this may not be possible, it should always be the teacher's goal. A shared understanding of the plans makes misunderstandings between home and school a lot less likely. Also, parents can often share information about the student that the teacher may not otherwise know but that could prove helpful in class.
- The teacher should share the student progress chart for every action plan with parents to keep them in the loop.
- If the student behaves in a particularly egregious manner, the teacher should call the parents before the student has a chance to misrepresent the incident.
- The teacher should ask parents early on how often they would like to be called about lesser misbehavior: whereas some have a hard time hearing about every bad choice their child makes, others want to know everything.

Teachers may also wish to share the following tips from Douglas Riley (1997) with parents for use at home:

- Do not take the child's behavior personally.
- Remember that you're the parent and the child is the child.
- You own everything in the house.

- The child doesn't set the standards for the family, you do.
- You must remain in control of yourself at all times.
- You should not be held hostage by threats from the child.
- Humor is more powerful than muscle.
- A child's attempt to gain power is healthy.
- You must be willing to make your child miserable (such as by administering predetermined consequences).

Although working with particularly challenging students is difficult, success in working with them is one of the biggest rewards a teacher can experience. Much of the success depends on having plans in place, working as a team with school personnel and the parents, and monitoring and adjusting the plans as needed.

CHAPTER NINE

Answers to Frequently Asked Questions

The following is a list of questions that we frequently get from teachers and administrators concerning our component-driven discipline framework.

Monitoring Questions

Q: **We teach in a middle school, and our students' behaviors in the halls between class periods is terrible. Teachers stay in their classrooms while students run over each other and often get hurt. What should happen?**

A: Ideally, your school should have a discipline committee that routinely checks up with teachers regarding ongoing concerns. Whether this is the case or not, the issue of misbehavior between class periods needs to be brought to the administration's attention, and a plan needs to be put in place to correct the problem. One possible plan would be for teachers to stand by the door during class transitions and monitor students. Perhaps a hall supervision schedule can be developed.

Q: **Although there is fairly good supervision at our school, some "nooks and crannies" of the building are difficult to monitor. What do you suggest?**

A: If your school has specific areas that are especially hard to monitor, the areas should be identified and staff members assigned to them. Ideally, cameras should be installed in such areas.

Q: At our school, certain students just leave the classroom without permission and roam the school without consequences. What should we do to change this type of behavior?

A: Students should never be allowed to leave the classroom without permission. Every classroom should have a hallway pass that is easily recognizable to everyone. Students spotted in the hallway without passes during class hours need to be reported to the office.

Relationships Questions

Q: What can I do about the student who just shuts down and does not even try to answer a question when I call on her? How can I get her to at least try to answer a question?

A: When students fail to even try to answer a question, it is usually because they are afraid of looking stupid in the eyes of the other students. It is important to make every attempt to ask these students questions that they know they can answer and then reward them for doing so. Sometimes a hint or clue for a student who is struggling with an answer can provide that little bit of extra support they need. If the student answers, "I don't know," say something like, "Well, if you did know, what might your answer be?"

Q: Some teachers in our building have yet to figure out that they are not kids. They dress, act, and talk like students. Everyone knows who these teachers are, and we want these behaviors to stop. What can we do about this?

A: This seems to be a problem in many schools. These teachers also tend to ignore rules if the students don't like them, or fail to enforce rules with their favorite students. Ultimately, it is the administrators' responsibility to deal with this issue. There is nothing wrong with discussing the problem with the principal and letting him or her know that it is hurting staff morale and disrupting discipline.

Parameters Questions

Q: What should I do when I give a student a response opportunity, but other students answer first?

A: When teaching your academic rules of conduct, you should let your students know that they will each have all the time they need to answer a question. This means every student is to remain quiet until he or she is called upon. If this lesson is not formally taught, students will be uncomfortable and will have a tendency to blurt out answers for other students.

Q: What can I do when students show me that they have forgotten the rules of conduct that I taught them at the beginning of the year?

A: Whenever the students show you by their actions that they have forgotten your rules of conduct, you must teach them again—whether it's the first week, the fourth month, or the last month of school.

Q: When students enter my room in the morning, they always appear to be out of control and somewhat disruptive. This behavior affects my ability to begin the class.

A: If students do not see the teacher immediately when entering the classroom, they tend to become disruptive. It is therefore critical that you stand by the door to greet your students as they enter and direct them to whatever warm-up activity you have prepared. Remember that active students are much less likely to get into trouble. Teach them that the bell does not start the class, you do, and that academics are to start the minute they enter the classroom. They are to get their drinks and sharpen their pencils as they enter or exit the room, not during the lesson.

Consequences Questions

Q: What if four out of five school days are extended so that students and staff members are staying at school until 5:00? How is it possible to run after-school detention with a schedule like this?

A: In this type of situation, you can run after-school detention once a week, on the early dismissal day. Then, instead of having Friday school as another option, you could run Saturday school for offenses that ordinarily would warrant Friday school. However, we believe that a better option is to still run after-school detention every day. This approach will make for very long days, but if the student has done something serious enough to warrant a detention, it should be administered as close to the offense as possible. This approach may require creative staffing and transportation home for these students—staff members need to be aware of the dangers of students walking home after dark. Parents need to be reminded of the importance of picking up their student as soon as detention is completed.

Q: What can we do when we know our school's system of consequences is ineffective, but our principal does not accept or understand this?

A: You've got to sit down with your principal and let him or her know that it is very difficult for teachers to do their jobs without an effective system of consequences. The principal also needs to know that teachers are willing to help implement such a system. Administrators are more willing to listen to concerns when viable solutions are recommended.

Q: The staff feels that it is important for the building to implement an after-school detention program, but some parents won't support this concept. What can we do about this?

A: The truth is that no consequence will ever be supported by every parent. The key to getting parent support is to involve parent representatives in the policymaking process as appropriate—perhaps even having them on the discipline committee, at least during the policy-formation phase. This way parents can hear the challenges that teachers face on a daily basis, and teachers can hear parents' concerns and ideas. In addition, parents can help "sell" the final product to other parents in the school community. Most parents respond well to logic, so schools should thoroughly review the rationale for after-school detention with them.

Q: When I give my students a consequence, they don't seem to care. They just continue to display the inappropriate behavior. What should I do?

A: Examine your consequences and ask yourself if they are meaningful deterrents to inappropriate behavior. If staff members are building positive relations with their students, teaching their parameters of appropriate behavior, and monitoring their students on a proactive basis, and the students are continuing to violate their rules, there is a strong likelihood that the problem lies with the consequences themselves. When students do not care about a consequence, this is typically because they believe they can skip it, or because it is not timely or meaningful.

Q: How important is it to communicate consequences to our parents? Should we seek "buy-in" from parents prior to going much deeper with our plans?

A: It's very important to begin the communication process with your parents prior to implementing consequences. Anytime you start something new, you're going to have some parents who don't support it. Uninformed parents can make the implementation process very difficult. The key is proactive communication. Meet with your PTA and tell them what you're doing and why. Call in parents who might not be on the PTA and explain what you're planning to do. Listen to their concerns and do your best to clear up misinformation or misperceptions. You should also discuss the discipline program with parents at back-to-school night and mail parents a copy of the plan (including the rationale for each consequence). Be certain to include the positive reward programs you are conducting as well, so that parents see that the focus is not on negative behaviors but on appropriate ones.

Q: What do you think about different grade levels having different criteria for processing and lunch detention? Should all grade levels be operating from the same criteria, or can they be grade level specific?

A: It can be perfectly appropriate to have different standards for primary and intermediate students, as they are at different stages developmentally. However, criteria must be consistent within a grade level—you don't want one 3rd grade teacher using a totally different set of referral standards for his or her students than another 3rd grade teacher.

Q: What can you say to your superintendent to get support for your school discipline program?

A: Remind the superintendent that parents as well as the school board demand that our schools maintain a structured, orderly environment. This goal requires a system of immediate and meaningful consequences, and parents who complain are not the majority, but a vocal minority. Reassure the superintendent that positive consequences are also in place and that the system is fair, consistent, and applied with respect.

Q: What can I say to parents who have concerns regarding the use of lunchroom detention for lunchroom infractions?

A: Let these parents know that it is incredibly difficult to maintain structure and order when there are only a few supervisors around to monitor a large number of students. Mention that without the threat of consequences, some students will throw food, run in the lunchroom, harass other students, and leave a mess.

Q: Should you communicate with parents about every processing and every lunchroom detention that a student receives?

A: Communication with parents is critical, but we need to be realistic. If staff members are required to contact parents every time they process a student or put a student into lunch detention, the consequence will not be untimely. Because these consequences are used for relatively minor infractions, we do not recommend requiring staff members to contact parents every time they are administered. If a student receives these consequences regularly, then parents should be contacted. Also, if parents request to be contacted whenever their students are disciplined, the request ought to be honored.

Q: How can we tell if the system of consequences is effective or not?

A: The school must compare the number of consequences administered over a year to the number administered in previous years. The discipline committee will want to reflect on this important information and use it to make adjustments in the overall system.

Q: How can you pay teachers for running lunch detention if you don't have a budget for it?

A: Lunch detention can be run by the principal or assistant principal. If a teacher has an extra planning period or break during the day, he or she can run detention then, or principals may give teachers reduced teaching schedules in order to free them up. If there is a supervision pay rate in the collective bargaining agreement, this could be a source of funding.

Q: What can I do when a student is processed into my classroom and the other students become upset and disruptive as a result?

A: If this happens, it is most likely due to ineffective classroom management in the classroom. One student entering a room should not set off the entire class. Students should be taught to ignore students who are processed into the classroom.

Q: What are some general guidelines and goals I should remember when selecting a consequence for students who violate rules?

A: The rule of thumb is to try solving the problem at the lowest level possible. Too many teachers will "use an anvil to kill an ant" when selecting a consequence. The lowest level of intervention is a nonverbal intervention, such as use of proximity or a moment of silence.

Q: Many students talk out inappropriately in my class, even though they know it's a violation of my classroom rules. What can I do to stop this from happening?

A: If you've taught this rule to the students and they choose to break the policy anyway, it's usually because the students believe they have nothing worthwhile to lose by violating the rule. Examine your system of consequences and ask yourself why it doesn't serve as a deterrent.

Q: What if there are a couple of teachers who never follow the school discipline program?

A: Ensuring enforcement is an administrative responsibility, so the principal should remind the offending teachers of this. If a teacher wants to discuss possible changes to rules and policies, a discipline committee meeting or staff meeting would be an appropriate venue to share concerns. In the meantime, everyone must follow agreed-upon rules.

Questions About Behaviorally Challenging Students

Q: Some of my behaviorally challenging students respond to questions I ask them by acting disruptive or making smart-alecky statements. What can I do to stop this from happening?

A: Remember that most behaviorally challenging students do not believe it is cool to look stupid; they'd rather look "bad." So if you ask them questions that they have no hope of answering, they will act disruptive rather than even trying to answer. Bottom line: always ask questions that these students have a chance of answering.

Q: What should I do if I am dealing with one disruptive, confrontational student and another student joins in the disruption?

A: You should make it known at the beginning of the year that it is never acceptable to join in when a student is being disruptive. Let students know that if they do this, they will face serious consequences themselves, and let them know what these consequences potentially can be. If it does happen, quietly go up to the second student and whisper, "Please remember my rule about never joining in with a disruptive student. I'm sure you'll make the right decision. Thank you." This statement can serve as a warning, but then you'll need to follow through with an appropriate consequence if the student persists. At some point, if the situation gets out of hand, you may need to call the office for assistance. Taking this step should be the exception rather than the rule.

Q: I allow my students with ADHD to stand in the back of the room sometimes during lessons, because I know they learn better when they are allowed to move. However, my other students get jealous and want the same privileges. They also start to ostracize my ADHD students because of this special treatment. What can I do about this?

A: At the beginning of the year, say the following to your students: "I will always treat each and every one of you fairly, but I will not treat each of you the same. You need to understand that we are all different. We have different hair, skin, and eyes, and we all learn differently. My job as a teacher is to do everything within my power to help everyone learn. Because of that, I will at times give some students different work, and I will allow some students to behave differently than other students. This is not because they are special or better than anyone else. It's because some students learn differently than others."

Bibliography

Ashley, S. (2005). *ADD & ADHD answer book: The top 275 questions parents ask.* Naperville, IL: Sourcebooks.

Barkley, R. A. (1990). *Attention-deficit hyperactivity disorder: A handbook for diagnosis and treatment.* New York: Guilford Press.

Boyles, N. S., & Contadino, D. (1998). *The learning difference sourcebook.* Los Angeles: Lowell House.

Boynton, C., & Boynton, M. (2005). *The educator's guide to preventing and solving discipline problems.* Alexandria, VA: Association for Supervision and Curriculum Development.

Costa, A. L., & Garmston, R. J. (1994). *Cognitive coaching: A foundation for renaissance schools.* Norwood, MA: Christopher-Gordon Publishers.

Covey, S. R. (1989). *The seven habits of highly effective people: Powerful lessons in personal change.* New York: Fireside.

Covey, S. R. (2004). *The eighth habit: From effectiveness to greatness.* New York: Free Press.

Danielson, C. (1996). *Enhancing professional practice: A framework for teaching.* Alexandria, VA: Association for Supervision and Curriculum Development.

Glickman, C. D. (2002). *Leadership for learning: How to help teachers succeed.* Alexandria, VA: Association for Supervision and Curriculum Development.

Hagener, N. (2005). *The dance of defiance.* Scottsdale, AZ: Shamrock Books.

Hall, P., & Hall, N. (2003). *Educating oppositional and defiant children.* Alexandria, VA: Association for Supervision and Curriculum Development.

Lencioni, P. (2002). *The five dysfunctions of a team: A leadership fable.* New York: Jossey-Bass.

Levin, J., & Shanken-Kaye, J. (1996). *The self-control classroom: Understanding and managing the disruptive behavior of all students including students with ADHD.* Dubuque, IA: Kendall/Hunt Publishing.

Lewin, K. (1935). *A dynamic theory of personality: Selected papers.* New York: McGraw-Hill.

MacKenzie, R. J. (1996). *Setting limits in the classroom: How to move beyond the classroom dance of discipline.* Rocklin, CA: Prima Publishing.

Marzano, R. J. (2003). *Classroom management that works: Research-based strategies for every teacher.* Alexandria, VA: Association for Supervision and Curriculum Development.

Patterson, K., Grenny, J., McMillan, R., & Switzler, A. (2002). *Crucial conversations: Tools for talking when stakes are high.* New York: McGraw-Hill.

Patterson, K., Grenny, J., McMillan, R., & Switzler, A. (2005). *Crucial confrontations.* New York: McGraw-Hill.

Platt, A., Tripp, C. A., Ogden, W. R., & Fraser, R. F. (2000). *The skillful leader: Confronting mediocre teaching.* Acton, MA: Research for Better Teaching.

Rief, S. (1998). *The ADD/ADHD checklist: An easy reference for parents and teachers.* San Francisco: Jossey-Bass.

Rief, S. (2005). *How to reach and teach children with ADD/ADHD: Practical techniques, strategies, and interventions.* San Francisco: Jossey-Bass.

Riley, D. (1997). *The defiant child: A parent's guide to oppositional defiant disorder.* Dallas, TX: Taylor Publishing.

Zmuda, A., Kuklis, R., & Kline, E. (2004). *Transforming schools: Creating a culture of continuous improvement.* Alexandria, VA: Association for Supervision and Curriculum Development.

Index

Note: Information in figures is indicated by an italic *f*.

school action plans—for relationships—
(continued)
citizenship certificates, 36*f*
sample log entries, 35*f*
sample plan, 40*f*–41*f*
sample roster entries, 36*f*
sample staff interview form, 37*f*–38*f*
sample staff observation form, 39*f*
school discipline assessment
about, 20, 26
direct observations, 28, 29*f*
parents, 24*f*
primary students, 27*f*
secondary students, 25*f*–26*f*
staff, 21*f*–23*f*
staff interviews, 26, 28*f*
schoolwide discipline continuous
improvement cycle, 70*f*
special education services, 102
staff inter-relationships, 14*f*, 16
staff interview form, sample, 37*f*–38*f*, 48*f*
students. *See also* behavior parameters
behaviorally challenging, 102–104,
117–118
behavior problems, 101–102
discipline assessment survey, 25*f*–26*f*,
27*f*

students—*(continued)*
sample action plan, 104–106
student progress charts, 105–106*f*
student-teacher relationships, 15*f*, 16,
30–33
surveys, staff, 47*f*

teachers—action plans for
behavior parameters, 43–45
consequence delivery, 66–70, 68*f*
monitoring skills, 55–57, 56*f*
relationship improvement, 30–33
teachers—discipline self-assessment
about, 13–16
behavior parameters, 16, 17*f*
consequence delivery, 18–20, 19*f*
monitoring skills, 16, 18*f*
relationships, 14*f*–15*f*, 16
teachers—improvement plans for
about, 88–89
behavior parameter issues, 91–94, 95*f*
consequence delivery issues, 96–100,
99*f*
monitoring issues, 94–96, 97*f*
relationship issues, 89–91, 92*f*–93*f*

About the Authors

 **Mark Boynton** is a retired elementary and middle school principal, and has also been an elementary school teacher and counselor. He received his Master of Science in Education degree from Seattle University. In addition to helping individual schools assess their discipline plans, Mark has conducted more than 300 seminars throughout the United States and Canada.

 **Christine Boynton** has been a substitute teacher, speech pathologist, program director, elementary school principal, and assistant superintendent in a large school district. Christine received her Doctor of Philosophy in Educational Leadership degree from Seattle University. She currently teaches in the education program at the University of Washington, Tacoma, and conducts school discipline assessments around the United States with her husband, Mark.

Together, Mark and Christine are the authors of *The Educator's Guide to Preventing and Solving Discipline Problems* (ASCD, 2005). They can be reached by e-mail at mcboynton@aol.com, and their Web site can be found at www.mcboynton.com.

Related ASCD Resources

The Educator's Guide to Assessing and Improving School Discipline Programs

At the time of publication, the following ASCD resources were available; for the most up-to-date information about ASCD resources, go to www. ascd.org. ASCD stock numbers are noted in parentheses.

Audio

Ensuring a Safe and Orderly School Environment by Elaine Jones (2 CDs, #504106)

Strategies for Anger Management and Conflict Resolution: It's Everybody's Job by Bob Hanson (2 CDs, #504107)

Managing Ethnic Conflict by Suleiman Hamdan (CD, #502260)

Books

Beyond Discipline: From Compliance to Community by Alfie Kohn (#196075)

Bullying and Harassment: A Legal Guide for Educators by Kathleen Conn (#104147)

Connecting Character to Conduct: Helping Students Do the Right Things by Rita Stein, Roberta Richin, Richard Banyon, Francine Banyon, and Marc Stein (#100209)

The Respectful School: How Educators and Students can Conquer Hate and Harassment by Stephen L. Wessler and William Prebble (#103006)

Talk It Out: Conflict Resolution in the Elementary Classroom by Barbara Porro (#196018)

For more information, visit us on the World Wide Web (http://www.ascd. org), send an e-mail message to member@ascd.org, call the ASCD Service Center (1-800-933-ASCD or 703-578-9600, then press 2), send a fax to 703-575-5400, or write to Information Services, ASCD, 1703 N. Beauregard St., Alexandria, VA 22311-1714 USA.